Project Two: Conventional Lap Steel Guitar

Parts of a lap steel guitar

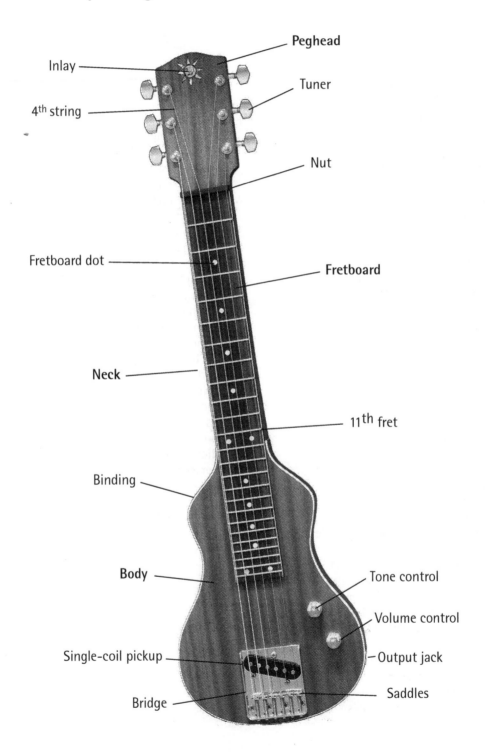

Inlay

Peghead

4th string

Tuner

Nut

Fretboard dot

Fretboard

Neck

11th fret

Binding

Body

Tone control

Volume control

Single-coil pickup

Output jack

Bridge

Saddles

It's easy to

Build Your Own Lap Steel Guitar

by Martin Koch

ISBN 3-901314-09-1
Published by Martin Koch, Gleisdorf, Austria

Copy editor: Franz Luttenberger
Layout, photos, line drawings and cover: Martin Koch

Check out this book's website

As a reader of this book you have access to an accompanying website at

http://www.BuildYourGuitar.com/lapsteel

Log in with

Username: `lapsteel`
Password: `1MiIhYbOlSg`

and find all the photos of this book in larger size and full color. You will also find printable templates and additional information like links to tools and parts suppliers there. You can memorize the password with the following sentence: "let Me in I have Your book On lap Steel guitars". Note that username and password are case-sensitive.

Table of contents

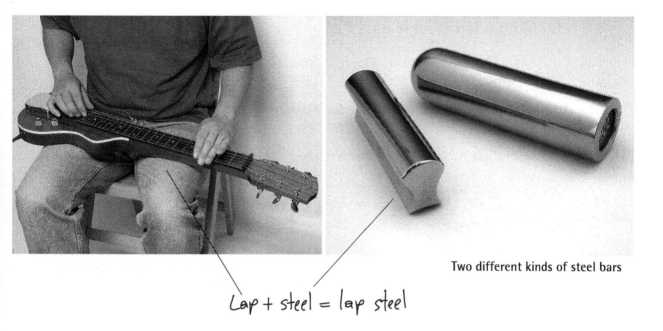

Two different kinds of steel bars

Lap + steel = lap steel

What is a lap steel guitar?

A lap steel guitar is a guitar with strings raised at the nut. It is put on the player's lap and played with a steel bar. If the player is standing, a lap steel guitar can be worn hanging on long straps in front of the belly, or it can be mounted on a stand. In principle any electric, acoustic or resonator guitar could be turned into a lap steel guitar by raising the strings with a special extension nut which fits over the existing nut. Apart from such modified guitars there are also genuine, purpose-made lap steel guitars with square necks. This book describes the building of two electric lap steel guitars. Because lap steel guitars are put on the lap, they can take almost any shape, from a simple square blank to a "proper-looking" guitar. Lap steels are usually tuned to an open tuning (i.e. the open strings are tuned to a chord). Two common lap steel tunings are open E and open G.

To tune a guitar to open E or open G, the standard tuning of three of its strings has to be altered. The standard guitar tuning, from the 1st (the thinnest, or treble e string) to the 6th string, is: e, h, g, d, A, E

Open E tuning
3rd string (g-string): tune one semitone up to g#
4th string (d-string): tune one whole note up to e
5th string (A-string): tune one whole note up to B

Open G tuning
1st string (e-string): tune one whole note down to d
5th string (A-string): tune one whole note down to G
6th string (E-string): tune one whole note down to D

Building a lap steel is easy

Making a lap steel guitar is a good way of "cutting one's teeth" in guitarbuilding. There are several factors why lap steels are relatively easy to build. In fact, the most difficult part will be to learn to play the instrument, but that's a different story.

Why building a lap steel guitar is easy

No round-shaping of the neck required
A lap steel neck can be left square because the player doesn't have to grab around it to play the instrument.

No fretboard required
Although most lap steel guitars do have a fretboard (made of wood or metal), the instrument can be played just as well without one. For better orientation the frets can be painted directly onto the neck.

No fretboard radius required
If you make a fretboard, you can leave it flat. A fretboard radius is a matter of comfort on a normal guitar that wouldn't make sense on a lap steel.

No truss rod needed
The neck of a lap steel guitar doesn't have to be comfortable. Since the hands don't have to grab around it, the neck can be left quite thick and square. Such a thick neck will not bend under string load, so there's no need for a truss rod to prevent or correct any neck bow.

No frets required
There are no frets needed to define an exact vibrating length for the strings. Lap steel guitars owe their special sound to the fact that the bar can be placed anywhere between the nut and the end of the fretboard. The strings of a lap steel guitar run quite high above the fretboard and never touch it.

No fret leveling and crowning required
To help the player with orientation it is helpful to have fret markers on the fretboard (or the neck). Often the frets are just strips of wood that are inlaid flush with the fretboard. Although not necessary, a lot of lap steel guitars still have frets, but merely for reasons of appearance. Since the action is high and the strings do not touch the fretboard, no leveling and crowning of frets is required.

No setting of the action necessary
The strings usually run $^{13}/_{32}$" (10mm) above the fretboard. There is no need for lengthy nut and saddle filing to achieve low string action. Fret buzzes are unknown to lap steel players.

No setting of the intonation

Because the strings are not pressed down on the fretboard when the guitar is played, there is no need for "setting the intonation". On conventional guitars, pressing down the strings results in a slight increase in pitch; to correct this effect, the scale length is increased by setting the string rests (saddles) on the bridge further back, a procedure commonly called "setting the intonation". On lap steel guitars all the saddles are placed at scale-length distance from the front of the nut.

Regardless of these numerous advantages, a lot of the steps involved are the same as in building a conventional guitar.

Measurement systems

A closer look at inches and millimeters

Understanding inches

I'm used to the metric measurement system because I grew up with it. Inches with their fractions of 1/16, 1/32 or 1/64 looked so strange to my eye that for a long time I never even tried to understand their meaning. When I forced myself to look more closely at the imperial measurement system, the mystery slowly got revealed.

Basically, all inch marks on a rule are broken up into smaller units based on divisions of two: 1", 1/2", 1/4", 1/8", 1/16", 1/32" and 1/64".

Fractions are always reduced to the lowest common denominator, i.e. 32/64" = 1/2". For longer distances the unit "feet" is used. 12 inches equals 1 foot.

Fraction terminology
In a fraction the numerator is the number above the line. In 1/32" the numerator is 1.
The denominator is the number below the line. In 1/32" the denominator is 32.

Understanding millimeters

Perhaps the same resistance I used to have against the imperial system will be felt by "imperial people" when looking at the metric system. In the metric system everything is divided into units of ten. 1 meter = 100 centimeters = 1000 millimeters. On a rule 1 centimeter is divided into 10 millimeters. On precision rulers the millimeter marks are divided up even further (0.5mm marks), and on calipers the finest division is 0.1mm (one tenth of a millimeter). The metric system is easy to understand because it is based on the decimal system.

Inches and millimeters compared

In practice, there are imperial precision rulers with 1/64" graduations available; metric precision rulers come with 0.5mm marks. It may be interesting to know that a 1/64" section (1/64" equals 0.4mm or, to be precise, 0.396875mm) is shorter than the finest division on a metric ruler - just for those (including myself) who think that inches are somewhat "coarser". On the other hand, it is easier to mark a distance of 53.3 millimeters than it is to mark a distance of 2.1 inches. You can easily estimate 0.3mm between the 53.0mm and the 53.5mm marks: it's

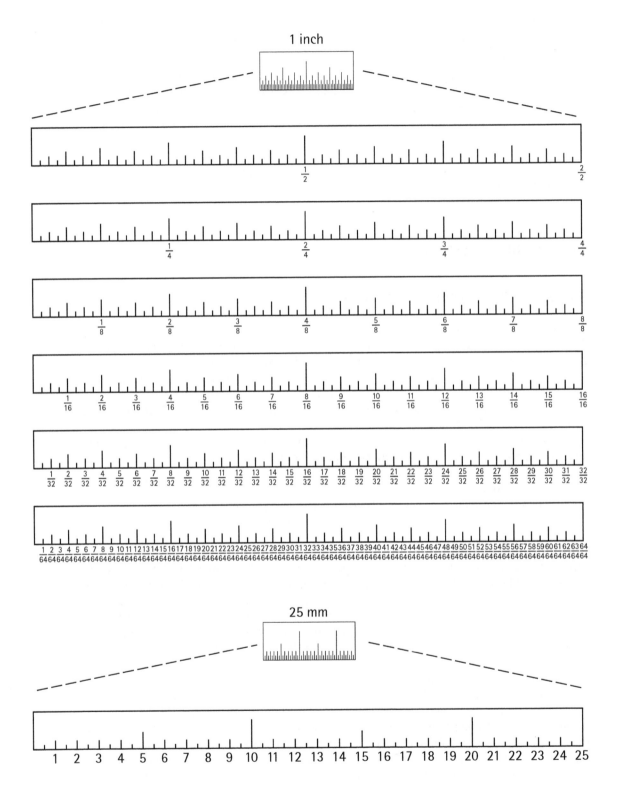

1 inch

$\frac{1}{2}$ $\frac{2}{2}$

$\frac{1}{4}$ $\frac{2}{4}$ $\frac{3}{4}$ $\frac{4}{4}$

$\frac{1}{8}$ $\frac{2}{8}$ $\frac{3}{8}$ $\frac{4}{8}$ $\frac{5}{8}$ $\frac{6}{8}$ $\frac{7}{8}$ $\frac{8}{8}$

$\frac{1}{16}$ $\frac{2}{16}$ $\frac{3}{16}$ $\frac{4}{16}$ $\frac{5}{16}$ $\frac{6}{16}$ $\frac{7}{16}$ $\frac{8}{16}$ $\frac{9}{16}$ $\frac{10}{16}$ $\frac{11}{16}$ $\frac{12}{16}$ $\frac{13}{16}$ $\frac{14}{16}$ $\frac{15}{16}$ $\frac{16}{16}$

$\frac{1}{32}$ $\frac{2}{32}$ $\frac{3}{32}$ $\frac{4}{32}$ $\frac{5}{32}$ $\frac{6}{32}$ $\frac{7}{32}$ $\frac{8}{32}$ $\frac{9}{32}$ $\frac{10}{32}$ $\frac{11}{32}$ $\frac{12}{32}$ $\frac{13}{32}$ $\frac{14}{32}$ $\frac{15}{32}$ $\frac{16}{32}$ $\frac{17}{32}$ $\frac{18}{32}$ $\frac{19}{32}$ $\frac{20}{32}$ $\frac{21}{32}$ $\frac{22}{32}$ $\frac{23}{32}$ $\frac{24}{32}$ $\frac{25}{32}$ $\frac{26}{32}$ $\frac{27}{32}$ $\frac{28}{32}$ $\frac{29}{32}$ $\frac{30}{32}$ $\frac{31}{32}$ $\frac{32}{32}$

1 2 3 4 5 6 7 8 9 10 11 12 13 14 15 16 17 18 19 20 21 22 23 24 25 26 27 28 29 30 31 32 33 34 35 36 37 38 39 40 41 42 43 44 45 46 47 48 49 50 51 52 53 54 55 56 57 58 59 60 61 62 63 64
64 64 64 64 64 64 64 64 64 64 64 64 64 64 64 64 64 64 64 64 64 64 64 64 64 64 64 64 64 64 64 64 64 64 64 64 64 64 64 64 64 64 64 64 64 64 64 64 64 64 64 64 64 64 64 64 64 64 64 64 64 64 64 64

25 mm

1 2 3 4 5 6 7 8 9 10 11 12 13 14 15 16 17 18 19 20 21 22 23 24 25

just past the halfway point (0.5/2=0.25) between the two marks. But how much is 0.1" on a ruler with 1/64" marks? To work that out, you have to take the additional step of multiplying 64 by 0.1, which is 6.4. Hence a distance of 2.1" is approx. 26/64" or 23/32". In some countries (Australia, for example) inches and millimeters are used on an equal basis.

A word on the inches and millimeters in this book

You will find both imperial and metric measurements used throughout this book, but they will not neccessarily be exact conversions. Although I am well aware of the fact that one inch is precisely 25.4mm and the correct conversion of 2" is 50.8mm, you will find length specifications like 2" (50mm) in this book. Whenever this is the case, please look at "your" number only and consider the numbers in brackets as intended for "metric people" only. If the exact measurement is not of such great importance, I see no point in telling you, for example, to make a piece of wood 313/4" (806.45mm) long. Better make it 32" long if you prefer inches and cut it off at 800mm if you're used to millimeters. This way everyone gets round numbers. Life is complicated enough, and I hope you don't mind if a guitar made on the basis of this book is about 1/2" longer if built in America. If you are used to both measurement systems, choose one at the beginning and then stick with it until the end; never mix them.

My tiny workshop

Measuring 10 x 4 feet (3 x 1.2 meters), the workshop I used for making the guitars in this book is really tiny. There's only room for a tools and material cupboard and a small workbench. Almost all my tools hang on the wall on magnetic tool holders. Although I would prefer to have a slightly wider room - say 6.5 feet (2 meters) - it is possible to build guitars in it. Such a tiny room also has its advantages (remember to be optimistic in life!). First of all, not having the space for power tools, I'm "forced" to use hand tools, which has turned out to be a very good learning experience. And then the limited space I have also means that there is absolutely no room for a mess: if I want to be able to do any work in my workshop, I have to tidy up regularly. This is good since no matter what I build, I'm always in danger of ending up in a heap of scrap and tools.

My workshop: a small room under a skylight

It's also very easy to control the humidity of such a small air volume: the room can be heated up in a very short time whenever lower humidity is required. For guitarbuilding, humidity should be below 50 percent.

Relative humidity
The amount of water air can hold depends on the air temperature: the higher it is, the more water it can hold. Relative humidity is the ratio between the actual amount of water contained in the air and the maximum amount it can hold at a given temperature. A relative humidity of 50 per cent in a room or out of doors therefore means that the air holds only half of the amount of water it could hold.

My small workbench

When I was looking for a small workbench I came across the bench shown below. It is manufactured by a small German company. The bench made of beech is of high quality and weighs about 60lbs (30kg). The top is 20" x 20" (500x500mm) in size. The only drawback of this small bench is its low steadiness compared to a full-size bench. Even when weighted with bricks it moves when a lot of force is applied during work. I can live with this, but if you want to build your own bench, you had better consider a larger top, e.g. 24" x 24" (600x600mm). My bench is held together by dowels and is not difficult to make. Just make sure to use well-seasoned beech or maple. You'll find appropriate bench clamping devices at woodworker supply stores. A cheaper alternative to this bench would be to mount a *Record* bench vise on a sturdy table.

My workbench

The bricks add weight to increase steadiness

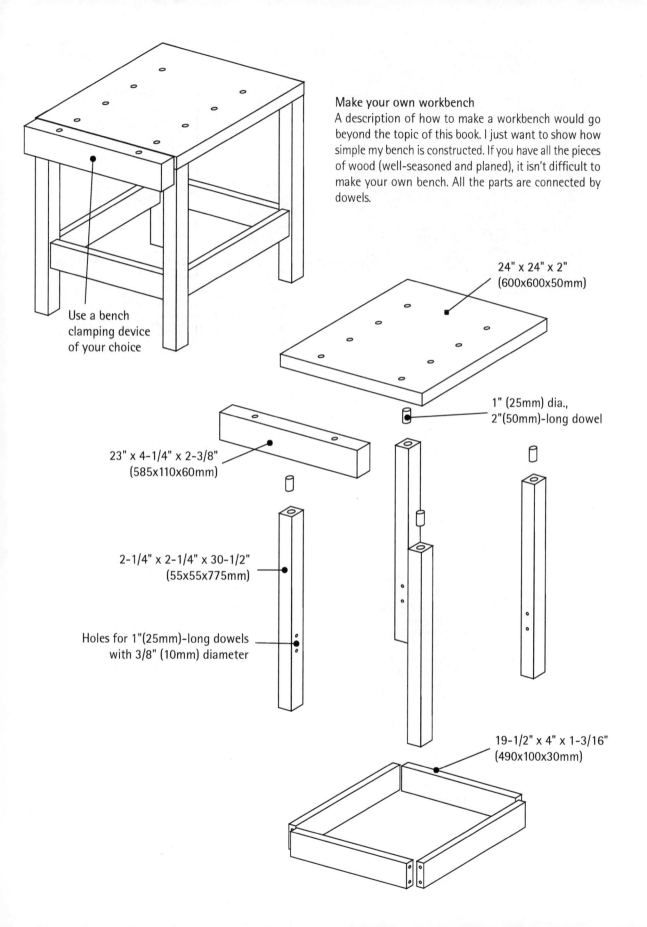

Make your own workbench
A description of how to make a workbench would go beyond the topic of this book. I just want to show how simple my bench is constructed. If you have all the pieces of wood (well-seasoned and planed), it isn't difficult to make your own bench. All the parts are connected by dowels.

Use a bench clamping device of your choice

24" x 24" x 2"
(600x600x50mm)

1" (25mm) dia.,
2"(50mm)-long dowel

23" x 4-1/4" x 2-3/8"
(585x110x60mm)

2-1/4" x 2-1/4" x 30-1/2"
(55x55x775mm)

Holes for 1"(25mm)-long dowels
with 3/8" (10mm) diameter

19-1/2" x 4" x 1-3/16"
(490x100x30mm)

Steel vise, height-adjustable and turnable

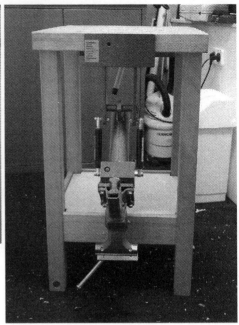

My vise

The vise can be folded away

I recommend that you buy a 360-degree swivel-base vise. Mine is a high-quality steel vise made by the German manufacturer *Heuer*. Also available for this vise is a lifting device that allows adjusting the work height. Because my bench is so small, I bought a much more expensive lifting model which allows folding the vise under the table when it is not needed. It is certainly expensive, but then again it's a lifelong investment. If you have enough room, you don't need the expensive fold-away function, but to be able to lift the vise is a nice feature I don't want to miss.

Record vise: Its jaw capacity can be doubled from 3½" to 7" (89 to 178mm) by removing the front jaw from the body and inserting it in the back (which is mounted on a 360-degree rotating base)

Parrot or Universal Vise: A very versatile vise used by a lot of guitarbuilders. It turns by 360 degrees and can also be mounted horizontally

Hand tools

You will find me using a lot of hand tools in this book, and not only because my small workshop doesn't allow for large power tools. I like hand tools and prefer them to power tools because I derive satisfaction and confidence from knowing what I can do by hand. Hand tools are much more quiet than their power-driven counterparts and most of them produce shavings instead of dust. To be honest, I have a fully-equipped, separate workshop with circular saw, jointer, thickness planer and bandsaw, but I didn't use any of them for building the guitars in this book. I prepared the wood blanks with my power tools, though. If you don't have access to the tools necessary for preparing the wood, buy it in ready-to-use form.

A word on tool quality

I try to buy quality tools. They may seem quite expensive at first, but they are a bargain when you consider how long you are going to enjoy them. Just take the example of the two manual riveting tools shown below, which I used for fastening case hardware with blind rivets. I bought the top one for about $15 and was able to install exactly six rivets before it broke - one part of a rivet had got stuck in the tool and had made it unuseable. Although I managed to repair it, I was fed up as I see little point in wasting my time repairing low-quality tools. When looking for a new one, I first boggled at the $50 charged for a professional tool and reached for another ($25) "pro" tool. But the $50 tool had a better leverage, and when I thought of the force that had been necessary to operate my first tool, I bought the more expensive one (which was described as extremely robust and came with a five-year warranty). I have never regretted my choice.

Two manual riveting tools
(Which is the high-quality one?)

Sharpening

To get maximum enjoyment from your hand tools, they should be properly sharpened. Newly-bought tools always need sharpening before first-time use and also at regular intervals later on in their lives. Fortunately, it takes only a few minutes to sharpen a tool by flattening two bevels so that the line where they meet (the cutting edge) is made as thin as possible. A dull cutting edge always has a certain radius, and it is this radius that has to be got rid of with the help of some abrasive material such as a stone.

Sharpening plane blades and chisels

Sharpening by hand

When sharpening by hand it is important to keep the angle at which the tool is held constant. I would therefore recommend the use of a good honing guide. One of the best currently available is manufactured by *Veritas* in Canada. An accessory makes it possible to hold short blades like those of spokeshaves or Japanese planes. A separate angle guide helps to clamp the blade to be sharpened at the correct angle. Unless you have a good reason to do so, never change the original angle of the tool.

Veritas honing guide system

Setting the bevel with the Veritas angle guide

Place the guide, together with the blade, on the first stone and move it back and forth while exerting a constant, light downward pressure on the blade bevel. Continue for about one minute, then switch to the next-finer stone. I use Japanese water stones and keep them stored in a box filled with water, so the stones are always ready to use. A dry Japanese stone has to be put into water for at least 10 minutes before it can be used.
Continue sharpening with progressively finer stones (e.g. 800, 1000, 4000, 6000 and finally 8000-grit). When you have finished, turn the blade over (i.e. put it on its flat side) and remove

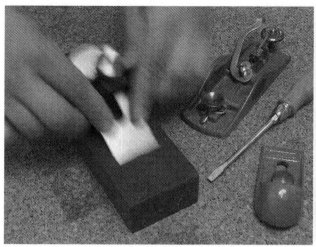 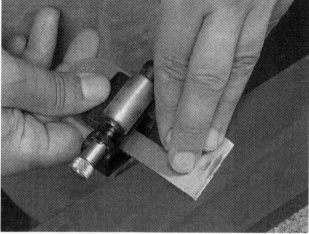

Sharpening on progressively finer stones   Removing the burr

the little burr which has formed during sharpening with circular movements of the even surface of the blade. Keep the 1000 to 8000-grit stones flat by periodically rubbing them against the coarse 800-grit stone. Flatten the 800-grit stone by rubbing it on 800-grit silicon-carbide paper placed on a sheet of glass. Apply water generously when flattening Japanese stones. Instead of using sharpening stones it is also possible to use silicon-carbide sandpaper: moisten a sheet of sandpaper, put it on a sheet of 1/4"(6mm) glass and then sharpen the tool as on a stone. Throw the paper away when dull. For in-between sharpening, 1200 and 2000-grit paper is needed; for coarser work and for sharpening new blades, start with 600 to 800-grit paper.

Sharpening with a machine
A machine that makes sharpening a breeze is the *Tormek* wet stone grinder. Even beginners will produce excellently sharpened tools with this simple machine. Several accessories are available for sharpening scissors, axes, lathe tools and so on. It's fun to work with this machine because the motor is very quiet. Its high price shouldn't put you off this useful, lifelong investment. There are also other wet stone grinders available, but the *Tormek* machine is the only one I know from experience.

Testing the sharpness
Hold a page of yesterday's newspaper with your thumb and index finger and move the blade close to your fingers over the edge of the paper. A dull blade will bend the paper, whereas a sharp one will cut it.

Using the Tormek wet stone grinder

Sharpening a scraper

Sharpening a rectangular scraper
When a scraper is new or its edge has become dull, the blade needs sharpening; this is normally done in four steps. There are guides and burnishing tools available which will help to keep the correct angles and make sharpening a scraper a breeze. A properly-sharpened scraper will produce fine shavings rather than dust.

Step one: Use a fine mill file to file the edges straight and square to the scraper surface as shown in the first picture on the facing page. To ensure that the file is square to the scraper clamp it into the bench vise.

Step two: Clamp a 1000-grit sharpening stone into the bench vise as shown in the second picture. Move the edge of the scraper against the stone, carefully removing all filing marks.

Step three: Remove the burr. To do this, lay the stone flat on the bench and move the scraper surface over it. When finished, the burr should have gone and the edge should be clean, straight and square.

Step four: Use a burnisher, a tool made of hardened round steel, to draw a burr along the edges. Remove the grease and put some oil on the edge; also put one drop of oil on the burnisher. Alternatively, you can apply some candle wax to the edges. Clamp the blade into the bench vise so that it projects over the table surface and then draw the burnisher along the edge, holding it horizontally and pressing it down all the time. Keep moving and turning the burnisher so that it wears off evenly. This will form a very fine burr suitable for fine work. If you need a less fine burr for coarser work, hold the burnisher at a slight angle (not more than 10 degrees) when drawing the burr. Repeat burnishing five to ten times, but remember to always work in the same direction. If you want to test the new burr, move over the scraper surface with a fingernail: at the edge, the movement of the nail should be slowed down by the burr.

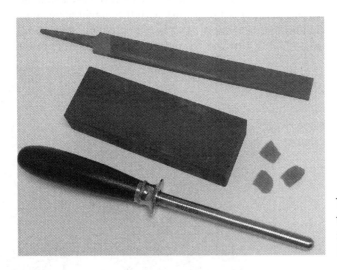

Tools for sharpening a scraper: fine mill file, 1000-grit sharpening stone, pieces of candle wax, burnisher

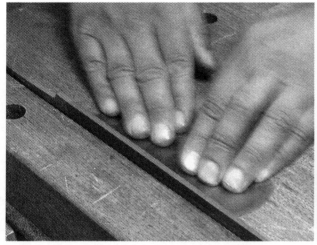

Squaring the edge with a mill file

Removing the file marks with a sharpening stone

Removing the burr

Drawing a new burr using a burnisher

Sharpening a curved scraper

Use a belt sander with 180-grit belt for squaring the sides. For the concave sections, use a small sanding drum in a drill press. Draw the burr as described above.

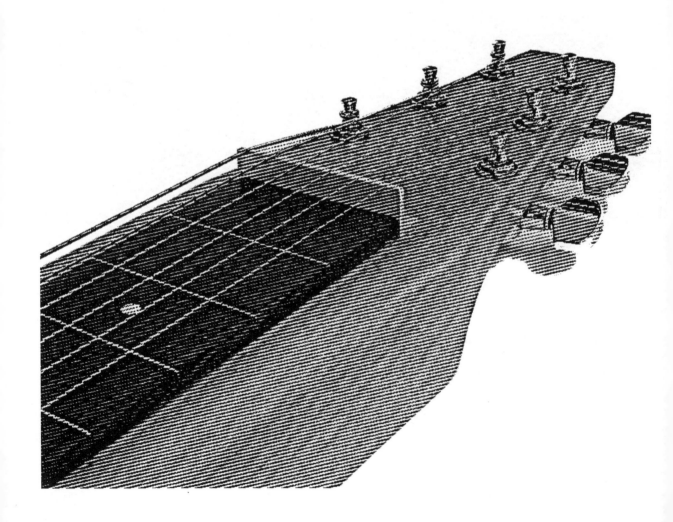

Project One:
Simple Lap Steel Guitar

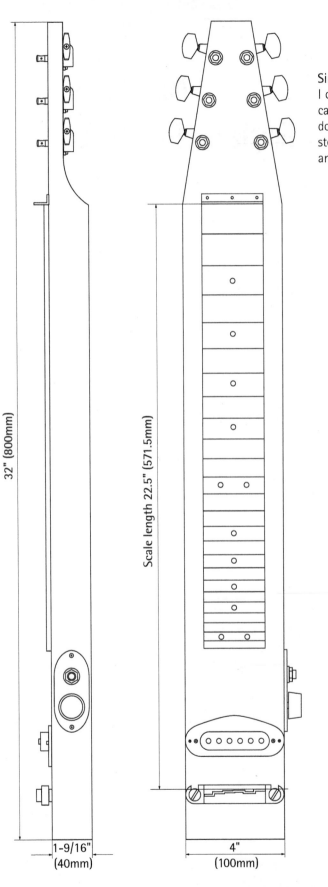

Simple lap steel guitar

I call this lap steel guitar simple because it is basically just a blank with strings attached. However, that doesn't mean that the instrument lacks anything a lap steel guitar needs, and it can be played just as well as any other lap steel instrument.

32" (800mm)

Scale length 22.5" (571.5mm)

1-9/16"
(40mm)

4"
(100mm)

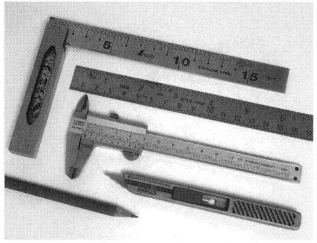

| Pencil, razor knife, caliper, ruler and square | Thickness gauges and pin marker |

List of tools used for Project One

Measuring and marking tools

Pencil: An ordinary pencil will do as long as you sharpen it regularly with a pencil sharpener.

Rule: An 18"(500mm)-long stainless steel rule is sufficient. The metric rule must have 0.5mm graduations and the imperial rule must have 1/64" marks over the entire length. If you want a high-quality rule, get a *Starrett*.

Square: Buy a quality square with 4"(100mm) blade.

Caliper: A quality caliper should be in every guitarbuilder's toolbox.

Thickness gauge: I use a Japanese-style thickness gauge. The excellent *Veritas* gauge is shown on the right in the picture above.

Cutting tools

Saws
Ryoba saw: I can really recommend that you buy a Japanese Ryoba saw. Japanese saws can have thin blades because their teeth cut on the pull stroke. There's no bending of the saw blade when the tool is used correctly. A Ryoba saw has two cutting edges: the fine teeth are for cutting across the grain, and the large teeth opposite speed things up considerably when cutting along the grain. Japanese saws are very popular among woodworkers, so it won't be difficult to find one at a good woodworking tools supplier. The only drawback I know of is that you have to blow away the saw dust rather frequently because there's always some there to cover the line you're following. Ryoba saws are held at a low angle to prevent scratching the surface with the teeth of the other side when making deeper cuts.

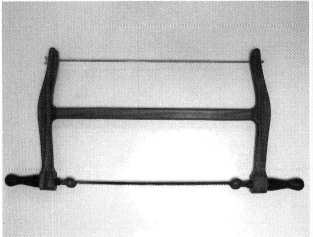

Bow saw

Hack saw

Chisels

Block plane

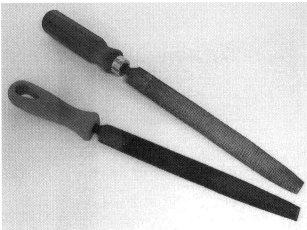

File and rasp

Rectangular and curved scraper

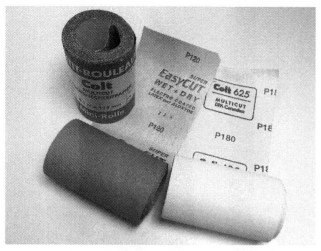

Sandpaper

Veritas sanding block

Bow saw: A small bow saw with narrow blade can be used in place of a band saw. My bow saw is a luxury model with Japanese-style blade. Such blades are available as spare parts and can be used if you want to make your own bow saw. For making one you need three hardwood battens, four wood dowels, a threaded rod, two wing nuts and two washers.

Hack saw: Another saw needed for cutting metal is a standard hack saw.

Chisels
One ½"(12mm) and one 1"(24mm)-wide chisel are needed for making the cavities.

Plane
A simple block plane will do for all the planing tasks of Project One. You can spend a fortune on planes, and the quality you get is certainly worth the money. If you want a reasonably-priced, well-made plane, get a *Record* block plane.

File, rasp
One fine mill file and one half-round rasp is needed.

Scraper
You need one rectangular and one curved scraper. Curved scrapers, like the one shown in the picture, are also called "goose-neck" scrapers.

Sandpaper
Get some 80-grit, 120-grit and 180-grit sheets (or small rolls) of sandpaper.

Sanding block
Also needed is a sanding block. The "Rolls Royce" of sanding blocks is made by the Canadian company *Veritas*.

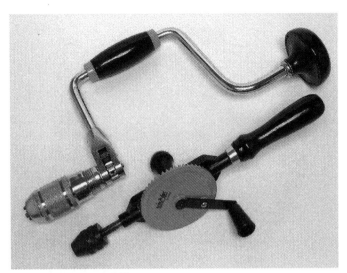
Brace and hand drill

Twist drill bit, brad-point bit
and Forstner-style bit

Boring tools

Hand drill
I use a hand drill for boring small holes up to ³/8" (9mm). With bits up to ¹/8" (3mm) in diameter the weight of the tool alone is sufficient to drive the bit into the wood. Just support the hand drill in a vertical position without applying any force on the handle.

Brace
Most braces are intended to be used with special-purpose, square-shanked bits. To be able to use conventional round-shanked drill bits look out for a brace with universal chuck. The chuck of my brace has four jaws. I even use 1"(25mm) Forstner bits with it. When the shank slips in the chuck, I'm applying too much force.

Drill bits
Twist drill bit: One ³/32"(1.5mm) bit (for pre-drilling screw holes) and one ¹/8"(3mm) bit are needed.

Brad-point drill bits: You need a 5mm bit for the inlay dots (ready-made dots usually come in metric sizes). Alternatively, you can use a ³/8" bit if you manage to get hold of dots of that diameter. A 10mm bit for the tuner holes and an 11mm one for the bridge posts are also required. I recommend that you use properly-sized bits. A 10mm drill bit is a must for every guitarbuilder as this is the tuner hole diameter required for the vast majority of tuners. If you live in the United States, you probably won't find 10mm or 11mm drill bits around the corner, but from browsing the websites of larger woodworking and tool suppliers I know that they are available.

Forstner bits: Buy a ³/4" and a 1" (20mm and 25mm) bit for removing material from the cavities. I have special sawtooth bits made for use in electric power drills, but they can obviously also be used, without electric power, in a brace.

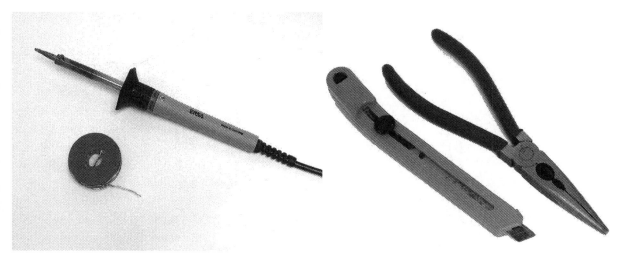

30-watt soldering iron and solder   A pair of pliers and knife

Tools for the electronics

Soldering iron: A 25 to 30-watt soldering iron is sufficient.
Pliers: A pair of combiation cutting pliers is needed for bending, cutting and holding wires.
Knife: Although there are a lot of different wire-stripping tools available, a normal paper knife will do for removing the insulation from the wire ends.

Special guitarbuilding tools

Nut files: If you want to do serious guitarbuilding, there's no way around expensive nut files. These special files, which are available from most suppliers of instrument-making tools, have teeth on their edges only and produce accurate, round-bottom nut slots. You don't have to buy all the different file sizes for making slots of different widths: wider slots can also be formed by simply rolling a file from side to side. The thinnest nut files available are as thin as saw blades and therefore very fragile. The following four file sizes would make a good starter set: .016"/ .025"/ .032"/ .042" (0.4 / 0.6 / 0.8 / 1mm). It is also possible to cut the slots with a saw first and to continue with a nut file.

Nut files: the files on the left are actually small saw blades of different cutting widths

Cam clamp

White glue, epoxy, CA glue, double-faced tape

Clamps

Cam clamps: All-wood cam clamps, such as the one shown above, are extremely popular among guitarbuilders. They are lightweight and apply sufficient, yet gentle force. Buy at least five of them for a start.

Glue
Wood glue: I used a widely-available white wood glue (PVA glue) for gluing on the fingerboard.
Epoxy: Epoxy is needed for gluing in the inlays. It comes in two parts, the epoxy resin and a hardener, which have to be mixed before use. Buy a type with a long open time.
Cyanoacrylate (CA) glue: One bottle or tube of thin CA glue (also known as "crazy glue") comes in handy for several tasks. Another name for this glue (especially in Europe) is "super glue".
Double-faced tape: Thin double-faced tape from the stationer's is very useful for various fastening jobs.

Materials

Wood

The guitar is made from one hardwood blank. I used maple, but you can, in principle, use any well-seasoned hardwood. Mahogany, walnut, cherry, oak, beech, alder, basswood could all be used just as well as any other tropical hardwood I may not even have heard of. Therefore, my standard answer to the question, "Can I use this particular type of wood?" is inevitably, "Why not? Give it a try." Although even softwood timbers like spruce or pine are conceivable, hardwood is preferable.
Each piece of wood sounds different, but it is practically impossible to predict exactly how. You would have to build several guitars and fit the same electronics, pickup and strings on all of them to be able to compare them. But why should you want to do that anyway? I'm sure you'll love the unique sound of your own, unique lap steel guitar.

Maple blank   Plum wood fretboard blank

Use dry wood only

The wood has to be dry before it can be used; otherwise it will warp and not maintain its shape over time. For instrument-making the moisture content should not exceed 8 percent (just in case that you have access to a wood moisture meter). There is a very simple method of making sure that the wood is dry enough: put it into a room where humidity is below 50% - this can be your workshop or any other room with constant humidity -, weigh the plank and note its weight and the date of weighing on it. Do this once a week until the weight remains constant (i.e. the piece doesn't lose any more weight). This is the point when the wood is in balance with the room and is ready for use.

Wood moisture content

The weight of a piece of wood always includes the weight of the water contained in it. The wood moisture content is the ratio between the weight of the water contained in wood and the weight of the fully-seasoned wood. The approximate wood moisture content can be determined with electronic measuring instruments measuring the electrical conductivity of wood, which is directly linked to the wood moisture content.

Wood needed

1 well-seasoned hardwood blank, 32" x 4", 1⁹/₁₆" thick (800x100mm, 40mm thick)
1 hardwood fretboard blank, 20" x 2¹/₂", ¹/₄" thick (500x65mm, 6mm thick)
1 piece of hardwood veneer, 8" x 1¹/₂", ¹/₆₄" thick (200x40mm, 3mm thick) for making the pickup and control cavity cover

"L" (left) tuner

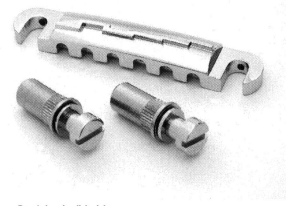

"Les Paul Junior" bridge

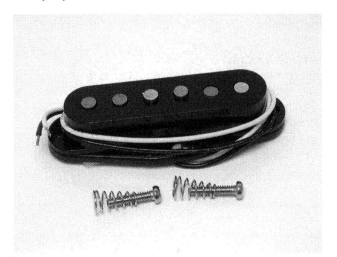

Single-coil pickup

Potentiometer

¼" output jack

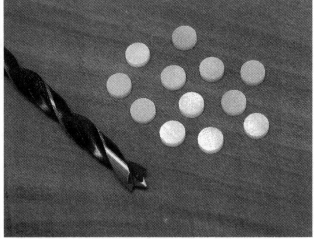

Inlay dots and brad-point drill bit of the same diameter

Hardware parts needed

3 "L" (left), 3 "R" (right) tuners
1 Les Paul Junior bridge
1 single-coil neck pickup
1 250K-ohm control potentiometer
1 knob
1 mono ¼" output jack
7 additional tuner mounting screws
12 white pearl dots, 13/64" (5mm) in diameter

Finishing materials

Danish Oil
With a 1-pint (0.5l) can of Danish Oil you will be able to finish several guitars.

Steel wool
"000", or, if you can find it, "0000" steel wool will do the final polishing.

Gloves
A pair of rubber gloves and hand cream - just in case you suffer from dry skin when wearing gloves - will protect your hands.

Rough calculation of material costs

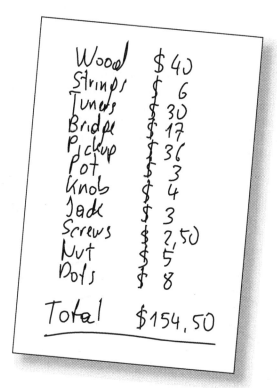

Wood $ 40
Strings $ 6
Tuners $ 30
Bridge $ 17
Pickup $ 36
Pot $ 3
Knob $ 4
Jack $ 3
Screws $ 2,50
Nut $ 5
Dots $ 8

Total $154,50

The marked peghead contour

Making the peghead

The peghead has to be made quite thin to allow mounting the tuners the conventional way (i.e. from the back of the peghead). Standard tuners can be mounted on 1/2" to 5/8"(13-16mm)-thick pegheads.

Marking the peghead contour

Choose one side on one end as the face side and then put the blank face down on the bench. Measure 5 1/2" (140mm) back from the end and pencil line **A** parallel to the end across the blank. Also mark this line on the sides of the blank. Set a marking gauge to 19/32" (15mm) and mark the peghead thickness (line **C**) up to line **A** on both sides and on the front of the blank.
Measure 180mm back from the end of the guitar blank and draw a line **B** parallel to the end all the way around the blank. Mark a round transition from the peghead to the body of the guitar on both sides. See if you can find a circular object with a diameter of 4" to 4 3/4" (100-120mm) that can be used as a template; a compact disk, for example, would be fine. I used a plastic cup with a diameter of approximately 110mm. Finally, draw a line at a distance of about 1/32" (1mm) from line C (i.e. 5/8" (16mm) under the face-surface of the peghead). This will be the line for the saw to follow.

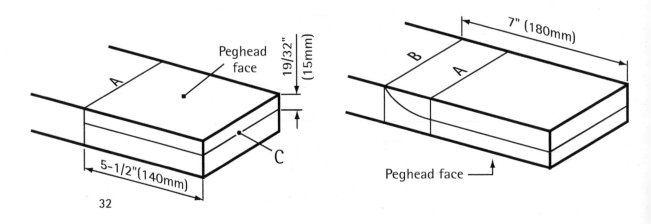

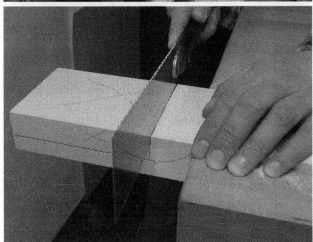

Above left: Hold the saw at an angle and cut just over the halfway point and halfway down; flip the blank over and do the same from the other side until both cuts meet at the top

Above: Remove the remaining material; hold the saw horizontally as you cut

Left: Remove most of the waste by cutting across the blank at line A

Cutting the peghead to shape

Clamp the blank upright into the workbench vise so that the guide line is perfectly vertical. Start the cut at one corner using the fine (cross-cut) teeth of the Ryoba saw. Hold the saw at an angle of 45 degrees and turn it over when the cut is about ¼" (6mm) deep. This cut goes along the grain and is therefore best done with the larger teeth of the saw. Don't force the saw and don't pull too hard, but hold it gently and hold it steeper (i.e. lower the handle side of the saw) with each stroke. The pulling action of the saw leaves the blade dead straight, making it easy to follow the guide line. Continue until you've cut just over the halfway point and halfway down. Then flip the blank over and do the same from the other side until both cuts meet at the top. From there saw downwards to remove the material in the center, holding the saw horizontally this time. Now that you have sawn halfway down the peghead, repeat the above cutting procedure once, sawing down to line A.

Remove most of the waste by cutting across the blank at line A. This is quite a simple cut, but you must take great care not to cut too deep. A piece of veneer or cardboard stuck into the kerf will protect the back of the peghead against scratches. If you use veneer of a contrasting color, the differently-colored saw dust will tell you when to stop cutting.

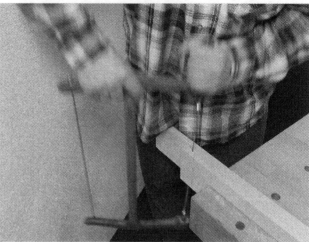

Cutting the concave transition

Now comes the most difficult cut: the concave transition to the full thickness of the blank. If you have access to a bandsaw with a narrow blade, this would be the ideal tool for the job. However, the old-fashioned bow saw will also do the same in a little more time. Clamp the blank to the workbench so that you can cut vertically. All cutting with a bow saw is done on the push stroke, with the teeth pointing away from you. Hold the saw with a light grip and let the blade do the work. Follow the guide line as close as possible, making sure it remains visible at all times. Also check frequently that the cut doesn't go astray at the bottom. If this happens, turn the blank over and correct the cut. With a bit of practice it is possible to make this cut in one pass. I had to turn the piece over and correct the cut several times, but was lucky because the blade had always entered the waste area. As you can see, the cut turned out reasonably well, just slightly off line B. If you have cut over the line, draw a new transition line and be more careful at the second attempt. There's some room for corrections; these will result in the bridge ending up a bit nearer the bridge-end of the blank.

Not too bad a cut, just slightly off line B

34

Smoothing the cut with a rasp ...

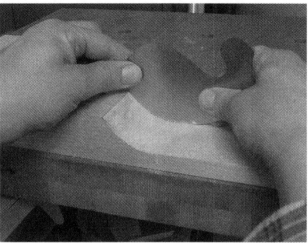
... and a "goose-neck" scraper

Marking high spots

Removing material from the higher areas

Smoothing the transition

Start smoothing and correcting the transition area with a half-round rasp, then continue with a "goose-neck" scraper until the surface is nearly smooth. Find a section on the scraper that resembles the curve of the transition. Continue on the back of the peghead, using a well-sharpened block plane to take off material in circular motions. Check the flatness quite frequently by laying on a square and looking for light gaps; mark all sections where no light shines through with pencil lines. By moving the square to different areas you'll get a good picture of where the high spots are. Take off material in those areas with circular strokes of the plane. The smoother the surface gets, the longer the pencil lines drawn on the wood will become. You don't need to work the edges as they are in the waste area (which will be cut off later).

Only the area between the two lines has to be perfect   Final cleaning of the surface

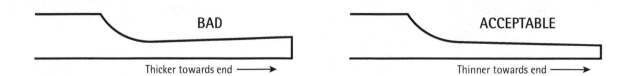

BAD   ACCEPTABLE

Thicker towards end ⟶   Thinner towards end ⟶

Measure 1¼" (30mm) from both sides on the top of the peghead and mark the approximate peghead contour to get an impression of where the important areas are. Pay attention to keeping a uniform thickness and continue smoothing until you get near the line marking the thickness of the peghead. At this stage you will probably have a hump in the transition area, where the flat part of the peghead ends and the round section starts. Depending on which one is higher, you'll have to remove material from either the flat or the round part until one flows into the other smoothly. As a last step use a rectangular scraper and work the entire surface, scraping with the grain until all the tool marks have disappeared. I ended up with a uniform peghead thickness of 9/16" (14mm). It is okay if the peghead becomes gradually thinner towards the end, but it doesn't look good if it gets thicker.

Cutting the peghead taper

If necessary, draw a new neck-peghead transition line B. Also mark a center line on the guitar block and draw two lines starting at a distance of 3/4" (20mm) on either side of the center line on the face of the peghead. Mark the peghead taper as shown in the drawing on the facing page. Holding the Ryoba saw at a tight angle, cut out the peghead close to the final shape. Smooth the surface with a block plane until you approach the line marking the peghead shape. Always work in the direction of the grain, i.e. towards the end of the peghead.

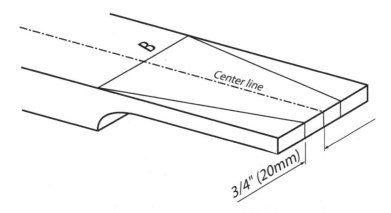

B

Center line

3/4" (20mm)

Cutting the peghead taper

Smoothing the cut with a block plane

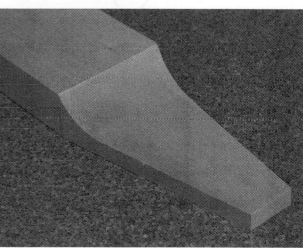

The smoothed back of the peghead

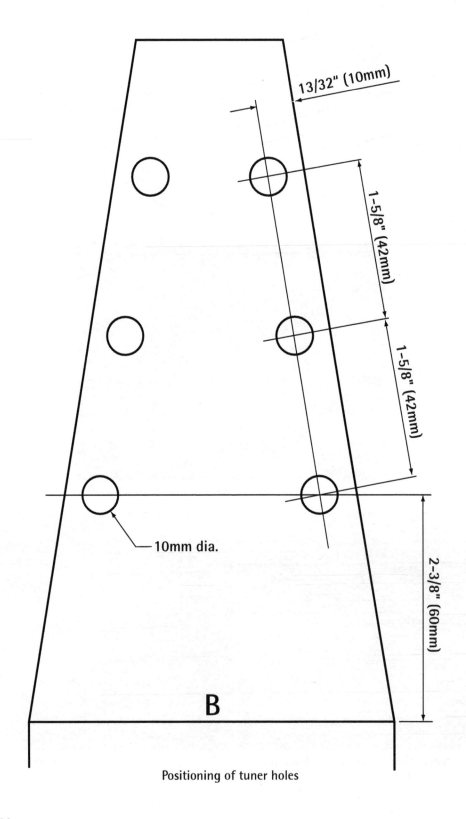

13/32" (10mm)

1-5/8" (42mm)

1-5/8" (42mm)

2-3/8" (60mm)

10mm dia.

B

Positioning of tuner holes

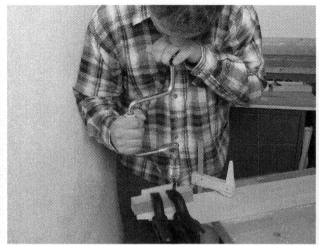

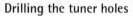
Drilling the tuner holes

Drilling the tuner holes

Measure the diameter of your tuner's mounting nut; this is the required tuner hole diameter (probably 10mm). Drilling the tuner holes is usually done on a drill press but can also be done by hand. To ensure that the holes are perpendicular to the peghead surface and to get the alignment and the distances between the holes right, I used a self-made drilling jig. If you mark and drill the holes carefully, you can get along without this jig. It consists of a 2" x 2" x 6" (50x50x150mm) hardwood block with three 10mm holes whose centers are 1⅝" (42mm) apart and ¹³/₃₂" (10mm) from one of its long edges. I have to admit that I went to a drill press for making this jig. With a piece of ¼"(6mm) plywood glued to one side as a guide it was easy to correctly align and fix the jig on the peghead.
The first tuner hole should be located 2⅜" (60mm) from line "B".
Position the jig and put a backing board on the back of the peghead before fixing the jig with two clamps. Make sure that the clamps stay clear of the tuner holes.
When using the brace I stabilize it by laying my chin on the back of my left hand. I drill with very little downward pressure and let the bit do the work.

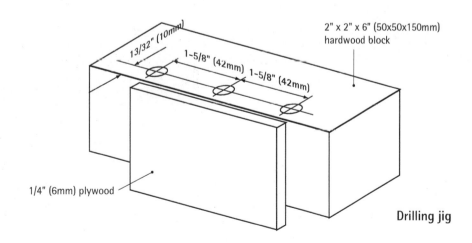
Drilling jig

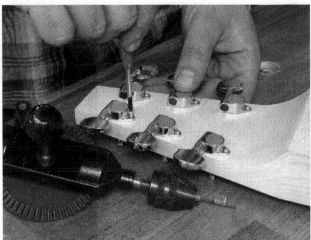

Fixing the tuners with the supplied screws

Tightening the tuner nut

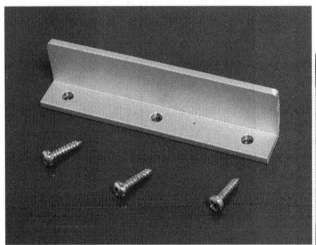

The finished aluminum nut

The nut is fastened centered and flush to line "B"

Mounting the hardware

Mounting the tuners

Fasten the mounting nut lightly and line up one row of tuners with the help of a rule. Pre-drill each hole for the small mounting screws with a 1/16"(1.5mm) bit and fix the tuners with the small screws. A piece of tape on the bit can serve as a visual depth stop to prevent drilling through the peghead. Then fasten the tuner mounting nuts. A common wrench size is 10mm.

Mounting the nut

The nut is a 2⁷/₁₆"(62mm)-long piece cut off a ⁵/₈" x ³/₈"(15x10mm) aluminum angle. In Germany and Austria such angles can be found in 1-meter-(3-foot) lengths in any DIY center. If it is difficult to get hold of them in other parts of the world, buy a larger angle and cut it to size with a hack saw. The thickness of the angle doesn't matter.
Drill three ³/₃₂"(2mm) holes into the ³/₈"(10mm)-wide side as shown in the drawing below. Align the nut on line "B", center it on the neck and fasten it with three tiny screws (see picture on facing page). I used the same screw type here as for mounting the tuners. These screws are about ³/₈" (10mm) long and approximately ³/₃₂" (2.2mm) in diameter. Pre-drill all the screw holes with a 1/16"(1.5mm) drill bit.

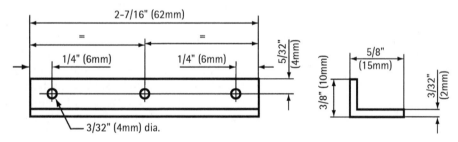

The nut, made from an aluminum angle

The holes for the threaded inserts   The mounted bridge

Positioning the bridge

The bridge is placed so that the saddle of the first string is at a distance of 22½" (571.5mm) from the front of the nut. I used a compensated bridge model (Les Paul Junior), but compensation is not an issue on a lap steel guitar as, in practice, intonation errors can be corrected by holding the steel bar at a slight angle when playing.

Measure a distance of 22½" (571.5mm) from the front of the nut and mark a line **S** perpendicular to the center line. Alternatively, you can also measure a distance of 11¼" (half the scale length) from the 12th fret. Take your bridge and measure distance **X** as shown below. Next, determine the diameter **D** of the string posts with a caliper. Subtract half of this diameter from measurement **X** to get the required distance from line **S**; this distance was 5/32" 4mm on my bridge model. If you work very accurately when marking and drilling the post holes, you can use this distance measurement and scribe line **P** parallel to line **S** and the bridge will sit right where it is meant to be. But because the whole bridge can be set further back with two allen screws, I recommend that you position the bridge (and draw line **P**) marginally closer to line **S** and then adjust the bridge to its exact position after mounting. I chose a distance of 1/8" (3mm).

Measure the distance between the two bridge posts and mark this distance centered to the neck on line **P**. My bridge posts are 81mm (3³/16") apart; another common value is 3¼" (82.55mm).

Measure the diameter of the threaded inserts. They are ribbed and you need the diameter without ribs (in my case 11mm). Drill two holes of that diameter, then tap the threaded inserts into place using a piece of wood between hammer and metal for protection.

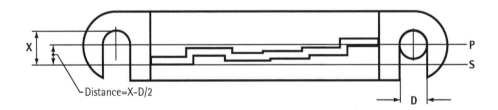

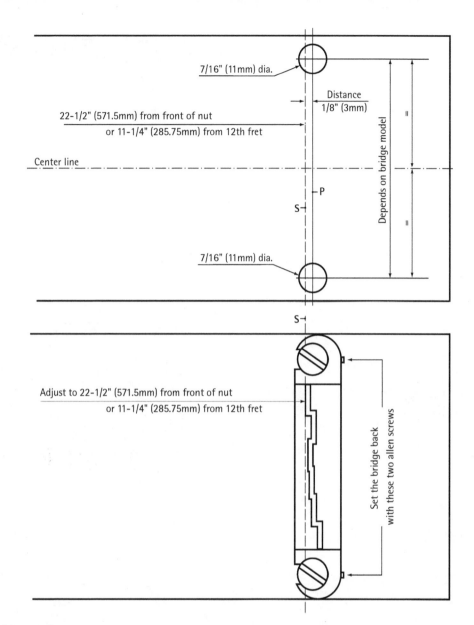

7/16" (11mm) dia.

Distance 1/8" (3mm)

22-1/2" (571.5mm) from front of nut
or 11-1/4" (285.75mm) from 12th fret

Center line

Depends on bridge model

P

S

7/16" (11mm) dia.

S

Adjust to 22-1/2" (571.5mm) from front of nut
or 11-1/4" (285.75mm) from 12th fret

Set the bridge back
with these two allen screws

A note on the bridge used

I chose the Les Paul Junior bridge for its simplicity and easy availability and because it can be adjusted higher than the usual Fender-style bridges. There's no extra stringholder required, and for mounting the bridge you just have to drill two holes.

It has two features which are not required on a lap steel guitar: (a) it is radiused, and (b) it has a (non-adjustable) compensation built in. This compensation can be corrected by holding the steel bar parallel to the fixed saddles (instead of parallel to the frets). There isn't any adjustment possibility to get rid of the 12" saddle radius, though. I solved the problem by filing small notches into all the saddles except the one for the 1st string. Cut the notches with nut files and deepen them until the tops of all the strings are at an equal height (see also page 58).

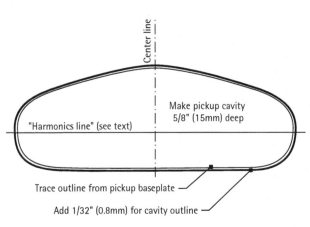

Center line

"Harmonics line" (see text)

Make pickup cavity
5/8" (15mm) deep

Trace outline from pickup baseplate

Add 1/32" (0.8mm) for cavity outline

The pre-drilled pickup cavity

Removing the remaining material with a chisel

Pre-drilling the control cavity

Cleaning up the cavity

Connecting the control cavity with the pickup cavity

Fitting the electronics

Cutting the pickup cavity

The only space available for mounting the pickup is the area between the end of the fretboard and the bridge. Lap steel guitars sound best when the pickup is placed close to the bridge as this gives a brighter sound. You can determine the best position by ear. String up the guitar and try to find points of rich harmonics. You probably know that one point with distinct harmonics is the halfway point on the scale. When you gently tap a finger on a string at the 12th fret and then pluck that string, you'll hear the harmonics right away. Now do the same closer to the bridge. It is more difficult to produce and hear the harmonics there, but if you try at different locations on the bass (sixth) string, you will be successful. Note any occurrences of harmonics with a pencil mark directly on the blank. I discovered harmonics 9^{31}/$_{64}$" (241mm) from the 12th fret on all three bass strings.

Remove the strings and mark a "harmonics line" across the plank. Then position the pickup so that the centers of its polepieces are exactly above this line. Also center the pickup on the plank, then lightly trace its outline on the wood. Add 1/32" (0.8mm) on all sides and draw the pickup cavity shape.

Cut most of the cavity with a 3/4"(20mm)-diameter Forstner drill bit, drilling to a depth of 5/8" (15mm). Remove the remaining material with 1"(24mm) and 1/2"(12mm)-wide chisels.

Cutting the control cavity

The control cavity is made on the side of the blank (see drawing below and pictures on following pages). Predrill a 30mm-deep and 60mm-long cavity with a 1"(25mm) Forstner drill bit and finish with a 1"(24mm)-wide chisel. Finally, use a 1/4"(6mm) bit for drilling a channel to connect the pickup cavity with the control cavity.

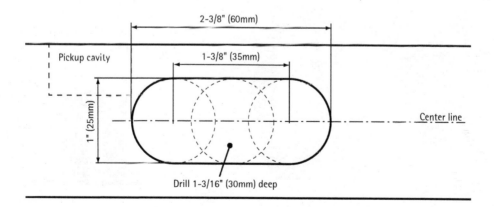

2-3/8" (60mm)

Pickup cavity

1-3/8" (35mm)

1" (25mm)

Center line

Drill 1-3/16" (30mm) deep

Making the pickup cavity and control cavity cover

Plane a 1⅝"(40mm)-wide and 8"(200mm)-long hardwood strip down to a thickness of ⅛"
(3mm). Mark the cover shapes on the strip as shown in the drawings below and cut them
out with the Ryoba saw. Drill through both ends of the pickup opening with a ¹¹⁄₁₆"(18mm)
Forstner drill bit and cut out the material in between with a fret saw; then file and sand all
the edges, closely following the drawn lines. This task looks quite easy, but I had to make three
pickup covers until I was satisfied with the look and fit of the cover.

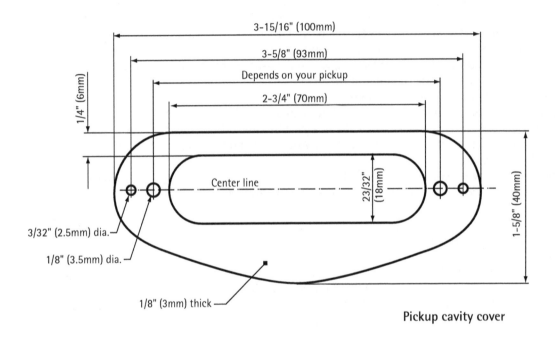

Pickup cavity cover

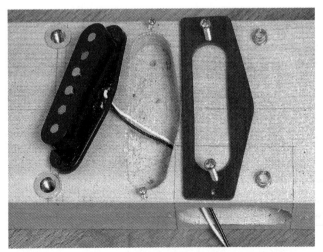

Small springs between pickup
baseplate and cover ensure
some tension for pickup height
adjustment

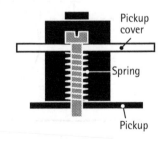

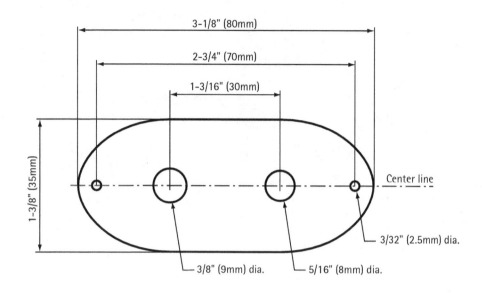

3-1/8" (80mm)

2-3/4" (70mm)

1-3/16" (30mm)

1-3/8" (35mm)

Center line

3/32" (2.5mm) dia.

3/8" (9mm) dia.

5/16" (8mm) dia.

Control cavity cover

Control cavity with cover

Plane one side of the fretboard blank dead-straight   Planing the fretboard blank to thickness

Making the fretboard

Plane one of the sides of the fretboard blank dead-straight, then the other; make sure the two sides remain parallel. The fretboard should be 2⁷/₁₆" (62mm) wide after planing.
Then plane one surface as flat as possible with a block plane. This will be the back of the fretboard (the gluing surface). Fretboard blanks from guitar shop suppliers have usually been prepared on a machine. If your blank already has a flat surface, better leave it alone; if necessary, go over it with the scraper.
Attach the back of the fretboard blank to your workbench with two long strips of double-faced tape. Then plane the top surface of the fretboard until it has a uniform thickness of ³/₁₆" to ¹/₄" (5-6mm).

Marking the fret positions

Using three small pieces of double-faced tape, fasten a rule parallel to one edge of the fretboard so that the zero-mark of the rule is about ¹/₈" (3mm) from one end. Cut the zero-mark into the fretboard surface with a razor knife and a square, then mark all the other (24) frets likewise. It is obviously impossible to work to an accuracy of one hundredth of a millimeter or one thousandth of an inch, so the figures will have to be rounded up (5-9) or down (1-4) to tenths of a millimeter or hundredths of an inch. Try to be as accurate as possible when laying out the frets. When you have marked the zero-fret and all other frets (plus an additional one for the fingerboard end), double-check the distances by reading each position off the rule and then comparing these values with the figures in the table. If the two differ by more than 0.3mm or 0.012", the mark has to be recut.
If you use a ruler with ¹/₆₄" marks, you may find the six "nearest fractions" columns in the table on the opposite page helpful. Simply add up the values of a line: the 14th fret, for example, is located at 12" plus ¹⁵/₃₂" plus ¹/₁₂₈" (¹/₁₂₈" being halfway between two ¹/₆₄" marks). The "Result" and "Error" columns show the small and insignificant deviations from the calculated values.

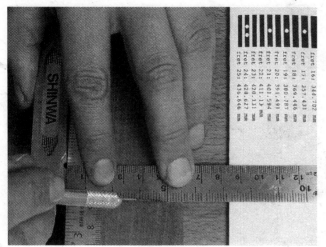

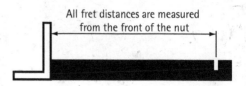

All fret distances are measured from the front of the nut

Marking the fret positions

Fret distances for a scale length of 22.5" (571.5mm)

Fret	All distances are measured from the front of the nut										
	Calculated values		Nearest fractions						Result	Error
	mm	inches	Full inches	4th	16th	32nd	64th	128th	inches	inches
1	32.08	1.263	1	1				1	1.258	0.005
2	62.35	2.455	2				29		2.453	0.002
3	90.93	3.580	3				37		3.578	0.002
4	117.90	4.642	4				41		4.641	0.001
5	143.36	5.644	5				41		5.641	0.003
6	167.39	6.590	6				38		6.594	0.004
7	190.07	7.483	7				31		7.484	0.001
8	211.48	8.326	8		5		21		8.328	0.002
9	231.69	9.121	9				7	1	9.117	0.004
10	250.76	9.872	9				56		9.875	0.003
11	268.76	10.581	10				37	1	10.586	0.005
12	285.75	11.250	11	1					11.250	0.000
13	301.79	11.881	11		14			1	11.883	0.002
14	316.93	12.477	12			15		1	12.477	0.000
15	331.22	13.040	13			1		1	13.039	0.001
16	344.70	13.571	13		9			1	13.570	0.001
17	357.43	14.072	14		1			1	14.070	0.002
18	369.45	14.545	14				35		14.547	0.002
19	380.79	14.992	14				63	1	14.992	0.001
20	391.49	15.413	15			13		1	15.414	0.001
21	401.59	15.811	15		13				15.813	0.002
22	411.13	16.186	16				12		16.188	0.002
23	420.13	16.541	16			17		1	16.539	0.002
24	428.63	16.875	16		14				16.875	0.000
25	436.65	17.191	17		3				17.188	0.003

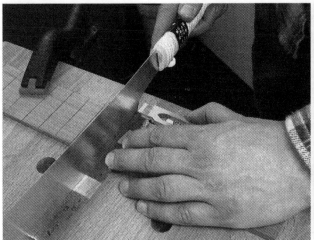

Cutting the fret slots

The taped-on stop allows cutting to a uniform depth

Cutting the fret slots

You can use any saw with fine teeth for cutting the fret slots. The slots will be filled with veneer strips later, so make sure to have veneer that fits tightly into the slots. Also note that the thickness of a saw blade is usually smaller than its width of cut. This is because most saws have set teeth, which means that they are slightly bent to the left or right. If your saw has a width of cut of 1mm, use 1mm-thick veneer. Because I wanted quite thin fret position markers, I used a saw with a width of cut of 0.024" (0.6mm). I can recommend veneer 1/32" to 1/16" (1 to 2mm) thick as it is much more stable (see facing page).

Cut the fret slots to a depth of about 1/16" (2mm). I attached a strip of wood to the underside of the square to ensure that the saw blade would touch the square above the teeth of the saw. This is more accurate and prevents the teeth from rubbing against steel and thus dulling.

When you have cut all the fret slots, deepen them to a uniform depth of 1/8" (3mm). A simple depth stop can help to achieve equal slot depth: tape a thin strip of wood to one side of the blade (use double-stick tape) so that it is parallel to, and at a distance of 1/8" (3mm) from, the tips of the teeth of the saw. Finally, cut through the fretboard at the zero-fret and the 25th fret.

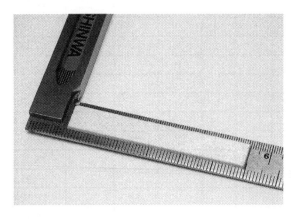

A strip of wood fastened to the underside of the square with double-faced tape raises its edge above the teeth of the saw

Filling the fret slots

I filled the fret slots with 0.024"(0.6mm)-thick veneer strips. These were so fragile that I had to stick them into the slots dry before applying a thin, liquid kind of CA glue (crazy glue or super glue) which flowed easily into the gaps on either side of the strips. Use wood glue for thicker types of veneer which can be pressed into the fret slots with the help of a clamp. Leave it all to dry for several hours; then take a chisel and cut the veneer strips flush to the fretboard surface. Take care not to mar the latter with the sharp edges of the chisel; better let the veneer protrude just a little and then finish the job with sandpaper.

Inserting the maple veneer strips into the slots

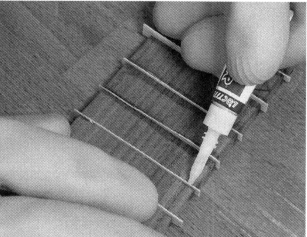

Applying thin CA glue

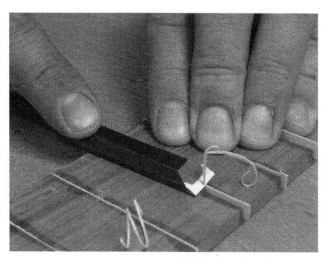

Cutting the "frets" flush

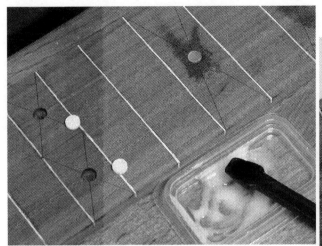

Gluing in the dot markers

The dots after flush-sanding

Fitting the fretboard dot markers

Orientation on the fretboard is made easier if you mark certain positions on it. Traditionally there are single dots before the 3rd, 5th, 7th and 9th fret and two dots before the 12th fret. This pattern is repeated after the 12th fret, i.e. there are single dots before the 15th, 17th, 19th and 21st fret and two dots before the 24th fret. The picture above (left) shows two lines drawn diagonally across one of the fret fields. I tried this method of finding the centers but would not recommend it as this way you will hardly end up with all the dots in line. Better mark a center line along the fretboard and find the centers between two frets by scribing one line diagonally across the fret fields.

The bit you use for drilling the cavities and the dot markers have to be of the same diameter (in my case 5mm). Since it is easier to sand the small dots flush than the entire fretboard surface, let the dots protrude a little when gluing them in. I used 1/16"(1.5mm)-thick dots, so I drilled to a depth of 0.050" (1.3mm). I did the drilling by hand, frequently checking the depth with a caliper. It wasn't difficult to get the depth of the cavities right. You have much more control over things when drilling by hand instead of using a handheld power drill.

For gluing in the dots combine two equal amounts of epoxy resign and hardener; use a type with an open time of several hours. Put a small amount into a cavity and press the dot in with the help of a dowel stick and a small hammer. Tap on the stick only very gently to not break the fragile inlay dots. Wipe off any excess glue with a damp rag and leave the epoxy to harden for at least 12 hours before flush-sanding the dots with 120-grit sandpaper.

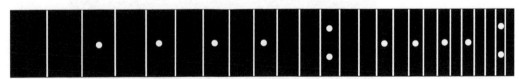

Typical arrangement of fretboard dots

Gluing on the fretboard

Now that the fretboard is finished it can be glued on the "neck". For this you need five to six clamps and a piece of wood slightly smaller than the fretboard to serve as a clamping caul. A caul is recommended because it distributes the pressure of the clamps evenly.

Apply a thin, uniform glue film on the back of the fretboard. I do this with my little finger so my other fingers remain clean. Place the board on the blank and butt it up against the nut. Then put the caul on top of it and tighten all the clamps a little. Increase the pressure on all the clamps in the row until they are all fully tightened. A clamp should ideally only exert downward pressure when tightened. There is, unfortunately, almost inevitably some other force involved which makes the fretboard move on the slippery glue coat. You can minimize this by clamping small pieces of wood to both sides and to the end of the fretboard. If you notice that the fretboard has slipped out of position and can no longer be moved, remove the clamps and the fretboard immediately, scrape the glue off carefully and start all over. I had to do this twice on this guitar until I discovered that it helps if you tighten every other clamp in the opposite direction, as shown in the picture below. Wipe off any glue that has been squeezed out with a damp rag.

Gluing on the fretboard

Finishing the guitar

Clean all the surfaces with a scraper, then sand the whole guitar with 120-grit paper. Vacuum-clean the surfaces and repeat sanding with 180-grit paper until all the scratches of the previous paper have gone; then remove any dust that may still be there with a vacuum cleaner. For rounding off the edges I used the 1/16"(1.5mm) *Veritas* cornering tool. This simple tool produces a nice and smooth corner radius when used with the grain.

I chose Danish Oil for finishing the guitar. Danish oil is an oil-varnish blend that is very easy to apply. It gives a nice, smooth finish with a satin sheen and sufficient protection against the wear a lap steel guitar is exposed to.

Veritas cornering tool in action

Danish Oil

Applying the oil

Wiping off the surplus

Finishing schedule

Day one:
Apply Danish Oil liberally to all surfaces with a rag or a brush. Wait for 5 minutes, then remove any surplus with a rag. No oil should remain on the surfaces. Leave the guitar to dry for at least eight hours.

Day two:
Repeat the procedure of day one.

Day three:
Apply a third coat of oil and rub the wet coat after 5 minutes with "000" or "0000" steel wool. Rub with the grain, then wipe off any remaining oil. One more night of drying and you can start assembling and stringing up the guitar.

Safety measure
Please note that oily rags can be dangerous: when wet, they can self-ignite by spontaneous reaction with the surrounding air. Used rags must therefore not be left lying around in the workshop but should be stored in an airtight glass container while waiting for the individual coats to dry. When they are no longer needed, they are best hung on a line and left to dry completely in an out-of-doors place before disposing of them.

Rubbing the wet oil coat with steel wool

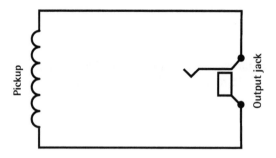

The simplest of all circuits: connect the pickup wires directly to the output jack

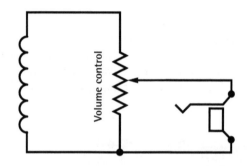

Circuit diagram: the function is clearly visible

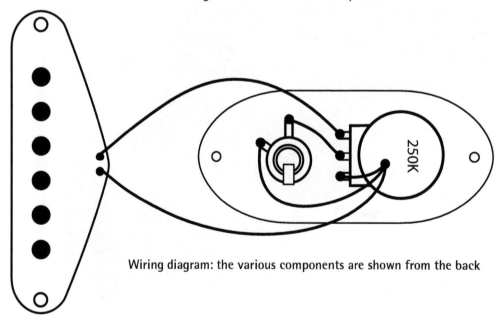

Wiring diagram: the various components are shown from the back

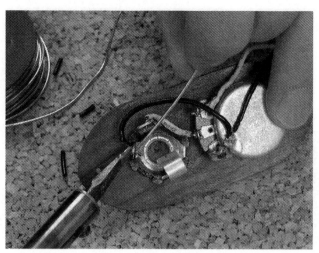

Soldering a wire to the short lug of the output jack

Assembling the guitar

Wiring the electronics

For this step you need a 25 to 30-watt soldering iron and solder. It is advisable to do all soldering in a well-ventilated room or near an open window and to avoid breathing in the smoke that is generated.

The simplest circuit would consist of just a pickup and an output jack. Wiring couldn't be simpler: solder one of the two pickup wires to the short lug and the other wire to the other lug, plug in your amp and start to play. With this type of circuit you have to adjust the volume on the amp. If you want to be able to do this directly on the guitar, you need a volume pot. Cut off both pickup wires about two inches from the end and remove the insulation over a length of ⅛" (3mm). Looking at the back of the pot, with its three lugs pointing towards you, solder one of the pickup wires to the left potentiometer lug. Soldering the joint should be done by heating for approximately three seconds and applying solder for two seconds (count in your head: "21, 22, 23" and "24, 25"). Then leave the joint to cool for half a minute. If heat is applied for too long, the pot may get destroyed. A good solder joint is shiny; if it is grey and ball-shaped, you have applied too little heat. In that case, re-heat the joint and apply another small amount of solder after a few seconds.

Use one of the above-mentioned wire cut-offs to connect the middle lug of the pot to the longer of the two output jack lugs and then solder one of the ends of the other cut-off piece of wire to the shorter jack lug. Connect the other end, together with the second pickup wire, to the right potentiometer lug. You can use the potentiometer case as a shield against ambient noise by bending the right potentiometer lug back so that it touches the case of the pot. Heat the connection thoroughly and apply solder. This connection is more difficult to make because the larger surface of the case draws the heat until it is evenly heated. Again, remember that you can destroy the pot by heating it for too long: it has thin conductive layers inside which can melt. For making this joint, limit soldering to a maximum of 10 seconds with a 30-watt iron. Instead of bending the lug back you can also use a short piece of wire to connect the lug with the case.

Cutting a notch for a string   Cutting the slot with a nut file

Putting the strings on

Thread the first string through the bridge, stretch it over the nut to the second tuner and bend it there. This ensures sufficient reserve for winding it three to four times around the first tuner post. Put the string up to the bend through the first tuner, start turning the peg with one hand while holding the string stretched with the other and wind the string on the post so that each new turn is placed below the previous one. Proceed similarly with the other strings. To get the required length reserve, always bend the strings towards the outside at the next tuner. For the two top tuners experience will tell you how much (approximately) you need to add.

Cutting the nut slots

Loosen the sixth and the first string and put them to the side of the nut. With a fine saw, cut notches for the two outer strings ⅛" (3mm) from the ends of the nut. Deepen and round the bass string notch with a proper nut file so that half of the string lies in the slot. The thin treble string is simply placed in the notch cut with the saw. Arrange the remainig four strings at the top of the nut so that the distances appear equal (i.e. put the thicker bass strings slightly further apart and the treble strings a bit closer together). Mark their positions on both sides with a sharp pencil. Notch and file the remaining slots so that the tops of all the strings are at an equal height (see page 43 on how to slot the bridge).

Slot the nut so that the tops of the strings are at equal height

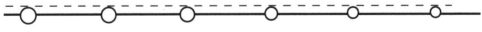

Slot the bridge so that the tops of the strings are at equal height

Final setup

Well, there's not much to set up on a lap steel guitar. As I have already mentioned, there is no truss rod to adjust, no frets to file, no action and no intonation to set. Check if the strings run parallel to the fretboard at a height of about 3/8" (10mm). If necessary, adjust the string height by raising the bridge. When adjusting the pickup height, remember to maintain a minimum distance from the strings: the gap between the top of the highest polepiece and the bottom of the string above it should not be smaller than 1/8" (3mm). If there is too much bass, you can set the bass side of the pickup further away from the strings.

That's all. **Enjoy your guitar**!

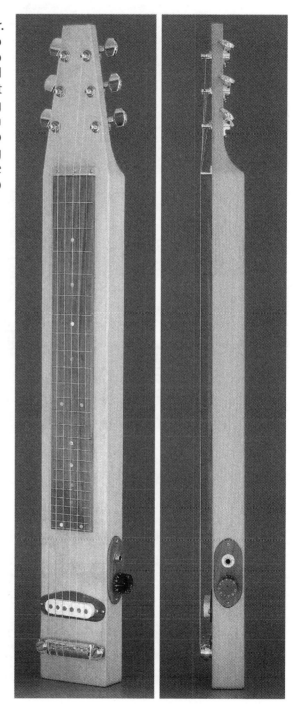

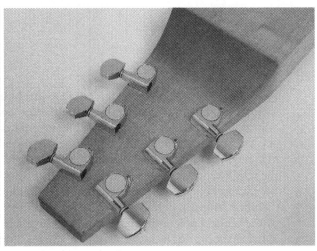
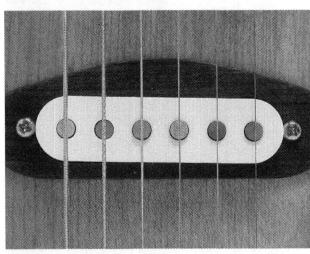

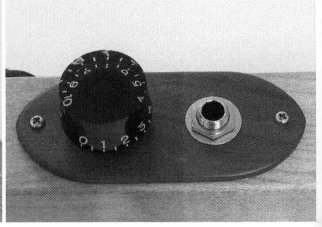

<table>
<tr><td>Gluing on the case top and bottom</td><td>Cutting the box apart</td></tr>
</table>

Gluing on the case top and bottom   Cutting the box apart

Making the case

I strongly recommend that you buy or make a case for every instrument you build. A simple, square case is not difficult to make and will protect your guitar. For the sides of the case you need one wooden batten (7ft x 3" x 3/8" = 2m long, 80mm wide, 10mm thick). Cut two 5⁵⁄₈"(142mm)-long and two 32¼"(820mm)-long pieces off it. I joined the edges at the corners with 1/8"(3mm) dowels. If you leave the dowels visible, this joint is really easy to make. Clamp one of the two long pieces vertically into the bench vise so that it is flush with the bench surface. Then place one of the shorter pieces at right angles to it and fix it with two clamps. Drill several 1/8"(3mm) holes through the wood into the face of the vertical piece. Remove the dust from the holes with a vacuum cleaner, put a drop of glue into each hole, hammer the dowels in and cut them flush with a saw. Do the same at the three remaining corners.

Use 5/32"(4mm)-thick fiberboard or plywood for the top and back of the case and glue both on simultaneously, with the case lying near a table edge. By placing a clamping batten across the case, as in the picture above, you can press on both sides with just one clamp and the whole gluing job can be done with as little as six clamps (the three clamps in the picture would have to be replaced with one clamp and a clamping caul).

Leave the glue to dry overnight. The next day, take a marking gauge and mark the thickness of the lid all around the case. You cannot just make two equal halves as, on the one side, there needs to be enough room for mounting the handle, and on the other, the upper parts of the hinges and locks, which are mounted on the lid, also require a certain height. When cutting the box apart, hold the Ryoba saw very flat (see picture above). The case hardware is fastened with small 1/8" x 3/8"(3x10mm) wood screws. I padded the case with 5/32"(4mm) cork sheets, but you can also use soft carpet pieces instead.

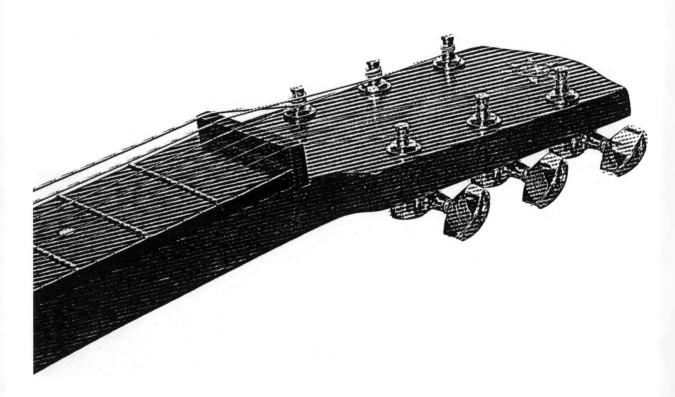

Project Two:
Conventional Lap Steel Guitar

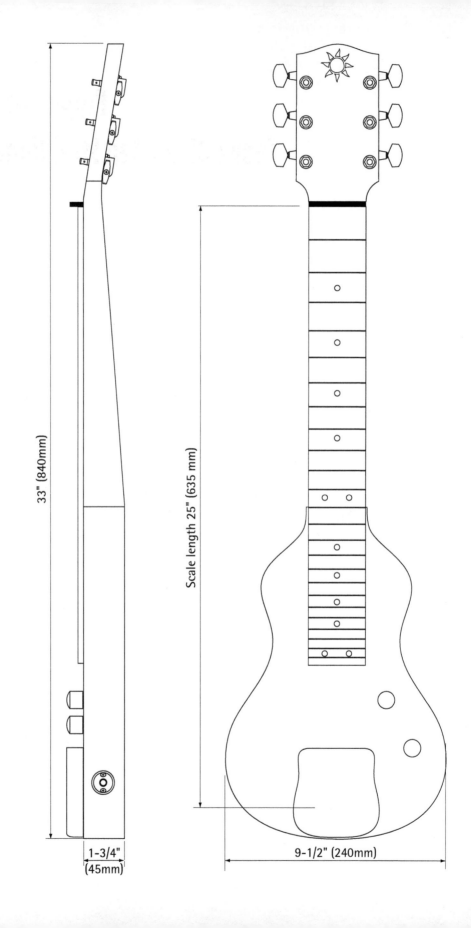

33" (840mm)

Scale length 25" (635 mm)

1-3/4"
(45mm)

9-1/2" (240mm)

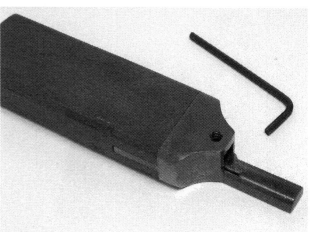

Purfling cutter

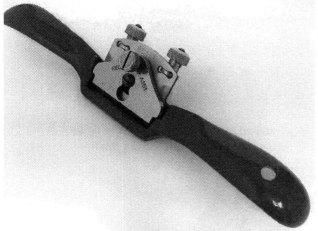

Router

Spokeshave

Tools, wood and parts needed

Tools

In addition to the tools used in Project One
you also need the following:

Measuring tools
Ruler: Unfortunately, an 18" rule is slightly too short for marking the 24th fret, which, on a 25" scale, is 18³/4" from the nut. You can mark it 6¹/4" up from the 12th fret, but with a 24" rule things are more comfortable.

Cutting tools
Spokeshave: A spokeshave with flat bottom is extremeley useful and one of my favorite tools.
Router: A router with a special bit is needed for making the binding rebate. Look for a good dust collection system when buying a router. You can use a plunge router or a fixed-base router. The reason why you find only plunge routers in my books is that fixed-base routers are not available in Europe.
Instead of using a router you can cut the binding rebate entirely by hand using a special purfling cutter and a small chisel. Such cutters are available from luthiers' suppliers.

Soft-face hammer and small Japanese hammer

My fret-end nipper made from a wire cutter
(I used a disc sander for removing the front bevels)

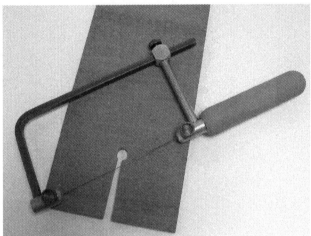

Pearl cutting saw and cutting board

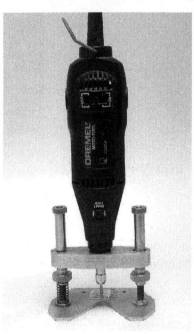

Small Dremel router
with special base

Tools for the electronics
Multimeter: You only need a measuring instrument for checking resistance if you intend to wind your own pickup. These days multimeters for measuring voltage, current, resistance, and even capacitance are inexpensive.

Fretting tools
Fret hammer: A soft-face hammer is needed for installing the frets.
Fret-end nipper: When the frets have been installed, their ends are cut off right at the edge of the fretboard with a special fret-end nipper (available from guitar shop suppliers) that cuts right at the tip. You can also use heavy-duty wire cutters with two bevels, but you'll have to remove more fret material by filing then. To avoid this, grind off the front bevels, as I did.

The guitar blank being glued up from two thinner boards

Rosewood fretboard blank

Tools for inlay work

Pearl cutting saw: If you want to embellish your guitar with pearl inlays, you need a jewelers's sawframe. Also buy several fine blades as they break quite easily. Unless your inlay is to have extremely fine details, medium pearl cutting blades will do.

Razor knife: Also needed for making the inlay is a razor knife.

Small router: The standard router for removing material from inlay cavities is the *Dremel Mototool* with a 1/32"(1mm) or even finer bit. There's a base available as an accessory which allows using it like a router; however, for more adjustment control I recommend that you get one of the special bases offered by luthiers' suppliers.

Wood needed

For this second project a mahogany blank 13/4" (45mm) thick, 40" (1 meter) long and 10" (250mm) wide at one end is needed. If you can't find one in these dimensions, you can glue one up from two or more 13/4"(45mm)-thick strips or from two thinner boards, as I did. With the first method you can build up the blank from one long strip and two shorter strips in the body area. I glued up the blank from one 3/4"(20mm)-thick and one 1"(25mm)-thick board after preparing the surfaces on a thickness planer. I used a lot of strong clamps for gluing.

The most sought-after mahogany type for building guitars is Honduras mahogany; however, due to over-exploitation it is difficult to get nowadays, and if you find some, it is going to be expensive. But relief: it doesn't really matter what type of mahogany from which part of the world you use - they're all pretty similar and they're all nicely colored when finished. I used some sort of African mahogany the name of which even the guy at the woodyard couldn't tell me.

You also need:

1 hardwood fretboard blank, 20" x 23/8", 1/4" thick (500x60mm, 6mm thick). I used rosewood.
1 hardwood veneer, 8" x 11/2", 1/8" thick (200x40mm, 3mm thick) for making the control cavity cover. I used ebony.

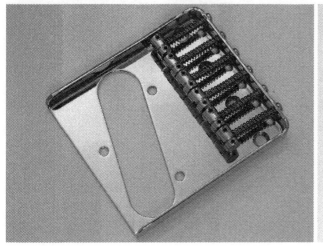

Telecaster bridge

Tele bridge cover

Mother of pearl and abalone shell blank

Additional parts needed

3 "L" (left), **3** "R" (right) tuners
1 *Telecaster* bridge
1 *Tele* bridge cover
1 *Telecaster* bridge pickup
2 250K-ohm control potentiometers
1 0.047 or 0.050mf capacitor
2 knobs
1 mono output jack
1 jack mount
6 guitar string ferrules
2 additional tuner mounting screws
1 small shell blank, 1" x 1½", 0.050" thick (25x40mm, 1.3mm thick)
6 feet or 24 pieces of medium fretwire
1 white celluloid binding, 0.06" x 54", ¼" high (1.5x1300mm, 6mm high)
1 black or black/white/black laminated celluloid binding, 0.06" x 54", ¼" high (1.5x1300mm, 6mm high)
12 white pearl dots, ¼" (6mm) in diameter

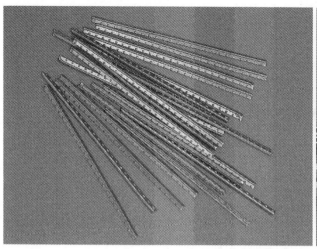

Pieces of fretwire

Binding material

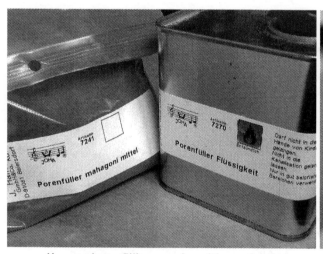

Hammerl porefilling powder with special thinner

Hammerl oil varnish

Finishing materials needed

Porefiller

Buy an oil-based porefiller of a color darker than the color of your mahogany. Most porefillers come in ready-to-use form in cans. I bought a porefilling powder and a special thinner, which I had to mix to a heavy-cream-like consistency immediately before use.

Varnish

A 1-pint (0.5l) can of oil-based varnish is more than sufficient. An excellent oil-varnish is manufactured by *Hammerl GmbH&Co.*, a German company shipping worldwide. The label on their high-quality varnish, specially designed for musical instruments, reads, "Öllack, Standard für Musikinstrumente" ("Varnish, standard quality, for musical instruments"). For an oil-varnish, Hammerl's "Öllack" dries quite fast.

Thinner: 1 pint (0.5l) of balsam turpentine for thinning the varnish and for cleaning the brush. Don't use mineral spirits. Balsam turpentine is made of tree resins and is, unlike mineral spirits, a natural product of high quality.

Brush: Buy a 2"(50mm)-wide quality brush with natural hair bristles. There are special brushes with bristles forming a tapered end which are particularly suited for applying varnish.

Jars: Three glass jars with lids of the same size. The opening should be wide enough to allow comfortable entering of the brush. The first jar is filled up to a quarter with balsam turpentine and is used for washing the brush. The second one is filled up to the height of the bristles of the brush and is used for storing the brush between coats. The third one serves as a replacement jar and only its lid is needed for the time being.

Sandpaper: 400-grit wet-or-dry sandpaper for leveling between coats; 600 and 1200-grit wet-or-dry sandpaper for final leveling; also needed is a small cork sanding block.

Polishing compound: Available from guitarbuilders' suppliers or in any auto body shop.

Gloves: A pair of rubber gloves and hand cream - just in case your skin gets dry from wearing gloves.

Rough calculation of material costs

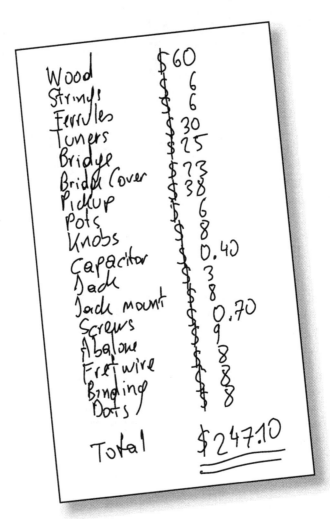

Wood	$60
Strings	6
Ferrules	6
Tuners	30
Bridge	25
Bridge Cover	??
Pickup	38
Pots	6
Knobs	8
Capacitor	0.40
Jack	3
Jack mount	8
Screws	0.70
Abalone	9
Fret wire	8
Binding	8
Dots	
Total	$247.10

Making the template

There is a guitar template drawing available from the website which accompanies this book (see page 3). When printing its three pages make sure not to check any scaling option in the printing dialog. After you've printed the pages, check if everything is in real-life size. Cut the pages as shown and glue them to the edge of a piece of cardboard. Cut out the template with a paper knife. Alternativeley, you can also enlarge the guitar shape drawing below. Draw a 1/2" x 1/2" grid on a large sheet of paper and transfer the guitar shape by estimating the positions between the grid lines. The distance between the "Nut" line and the "12th fret" line is half the scale length, i.e. 121/4" (317.5mm).

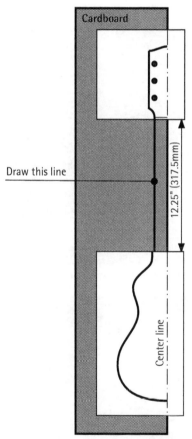

Arrange the drawings on cardboard,
then cut out the shape

Alternative to the printout:
enlarge this guitar shape drawing
so that one square equals 0.5" x 0.5"

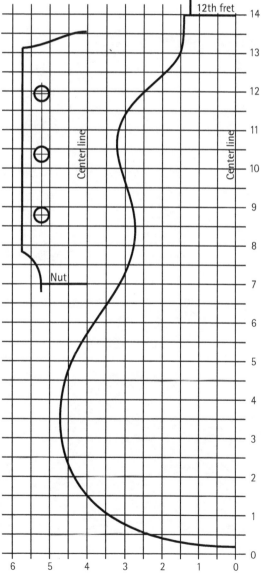

Transferring the outline to the wood

Cutting out the shape

Who said you needed a band saw?

Marking high spots using a square and a pencil

Removing material from the high spots with a rasp

Planing the angled peghead face

Cutting the back of the peghead

Removing the waste

Shaping the guitar

Waste

5/8"(15mm)-thick peghead

Waste

5/8" (15mm) drop off

Cutting out the shape

Draw a center line on the blank and transfer the guitar shape onto the wood using the cardboard template. Use a bandsaw or bow saw for cutting out the shape close to the line. If you cut by hand like me, fasten the blank on the edge of the workbench with the help of two clamps. Hold the saw lightly and so that it cuts on the push stroke.

Smoothing the cut
The cut might not turn out 100 percent perpendicular to the top surface in all areas. Mark all the high spots on the sides of the body every half inch or so by laying on a square as shown in the picture and drawing lines where no light gap is visible between wood and square. These lines are the high spots and show where material needs to be removed. Use a coarse rasp for this and continue until all the pencil lines have disappeared. Repeat marking and removing high spots. The surface doesn't have to be perfectly smooth at this point; just keep close to the contour line and correct any imperfect sections of the cut.

Cutting the peghead angle

Using the template, transfer the nut position onto the neck. The peghead of this guitar will be angled back by approximately 5 degrees. You don't need to measure the angle. Just mark a 5/8"(15mm) drop-off on both sides of the peghead, as shown in the drawing above. You could remove most of the waste with a saw, but I don't think it takes any longer with the block plane. Start planing at the end of the peghead and work your way up towards the nut. Make sure to keep parallel to the line.
Mark the peghead thickness of 5/8" (15mm) on the sides of the peghead and remove the waste with the Ryoba saw.

Cutting the back of the neck

Smoothing the back of the neck

Cutting the back of the neck

The back of the neck is cut so that it becomes gradually thinner towards the nut. I used a bow saw for cutting and started at the peghead end. Then I put a wider blade into the saw and continued cutting, assuming that the wider blade would make it easier to cut straight. Unfortunately, this turned out to be a mistake and I ended up off line because I hadn't taken enough care - the angled peghead and the wide blade had made it impossible to keep to the line. So I had to use the narrow blade again to correct the cut and ended up with a slight curve instead of a straight taper (which would have looked better and would also have been easier to plane). From experience I can therefore recommend a narrow blade for this cut. If you want to use a wider blade, start the cut at the body end, but bear in mind that you have to enter the wood at a very small angle there, which is quite difficult.

HOW IT SHOULD BE

HOW I ENDED UP

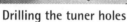
Drilling the tuner holes

Drilling the tuner holes

Measure the diameter of your tuner's mounting nut; this is the required tuner hole diameter (probably 10mm). Normally a drill press is used for drilling the tuner holes, but it can also be done by hand. To ensure that the holes are perpendicular to the peghead surface and to get the alignment and the distances between the holes right, I used a self-made drilling jig. It consists of a hardwood block with three 10mm(13/32") holes whose centers are 15/8" (42mm) apart and 13/32" (10mm) from one of its longer edges. You can find a drawing of this jig on page 39 in this book. I have to admit that I went to a drill press for making this jig. With a piece of plywood glued to one side as a guide it was easy to correctly align and fix the jig on the peghead.

The first hole should be located 2" (50mm) from the line where the peghead angle starts. Position the jig and put a backing board on the back of the peghead before fixing the jig with two clamps. Make sure that the clamps stay clear of the tuner holes. I used the waste part from cutting the back of the peghead as a backing board. Without such a board the edges of the holes would be torn out by the bit exiting the wood at the back of the peghead.

When using the brace I stabilize it by laying my chin on the back of my left hand. I drill with very little downward pressure and let the bit do the work. A sharp bit is essential. If the shaft of the drill bit slips into the chuck, you are using too much pressure.

Transferring the fret slot positions from a pre-slotted, ready-made fretboard

Making the fretboard

First plane one edge of the fretboard straight, then the other until the fretboard has a uniform width of 2³/8" (60mm). If you don't want to bind the fretboard, make it 2⁷/16" (62mm) wide. Tape the back of the fretboard to your workbench with two long strips of double-faced tape. Fretboard blanks from luthiers' suppliers are already machined and have flat surfaces. Use a block plane or a jack plane No4 to plane the fretboard blank to a thickness of ⁷/32" to ¹/4" (5 to 6mm). If you put a piece of wood of this thickness to different places at the side of the fretboard, you'll be able to tell if the board is uniformly thick in all areas. Finally, remove all plane marks from the surface with a scraper.

Marking the fret positions

You can mark the fret slot positions with the help of a rule (as described in Project One). To speed things up, I taped a pre-slotted, ready-made, 25"-scale fretboard alongside the fretboard blank and then transferred the fret slot positions to the blank with a square (picture above).

Determining the fret slot width

If you like, you can fill the fret slots with maple veneer (see Project One). I opted to have real frets on this guitar. Although frets are not required on a lap steel, I find it a bit easier to hammer frets into the slots than to fill them, cut the veneer flush and sand the surface. I used a 24-piece set of small fretwire, but you can also buy fretwire in 2-foot (600mm) straight lengths or in rolls. Make sure to have a saw with the right width of cut for your fretwire. Most frets require 0.022"(0.55mm)-wide slots, but to be sure measure the width of the tang (remove any burr that is left from the manufacturing process) with a caliper. A fret slot of exactly this width would be too narrow because of the barbs on the fretwire which help to keep the wire in place. Add about 10 percent to the tang width measurement and you'll have a good guide for choosing the saw.

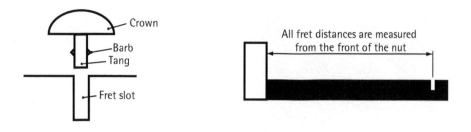

Fret distances for a scale length of 25" (635mm)

All distances are measured from the front of the nut										
Fret	Calculated values		Nearest fractions						Result	Error
	mm	inches	Full inches	4th	16th	32nd	64th	128th	inches	inches
1	35.64	1.403	1			13			1.406	0.003
2	69.28	2.728	2			23		1	2.727	0.001
3	101.03	3.978	3			31		1	3.977	0.001
4	131.00	5.158	5			5			5.156	0.002
5	159.29	6.271	6				17	1	6.273	0.002
6	185.99	7.322	7		5			1	7.320	0.002
7	211.19	8.315	8		5				8.313	0.002
8	234.98	9.251	9	1					9.250	0.001
9	257.43	10.135	10		2			1	10.133	0.002
10	278.62	10.969	10			31			10.969	0.000
11	298.62	11.757	11	3				1	11.758	0.001
12	317.50	12.500	12	2					12.500	0.000
13	335.32	13.202	13				13		13.203	0.001
14	352.14	13.864	13				55	1	13.867	0.003
15	368.02	14.489	14				31	1	14.492	0.003
16	383.00	15.079	15				5		15.078	0.001
17	397.15	15.636	15		10			1	15.633	0.003
18	410.50	16.161	16				10	1	16.164	0.003
19	423.10	16.657	16			21			16.656	0.001
20	434.99	17.126	17		2				17.125	0.001
21	446.22	17.568	17		9			1	17.570	0.002
22	456.81	17.985	17				63		17.984	0.001
23	466.81	18.378	18		6				18.375	0.003
24	476.25	18.750	18	3					18.750	0.000
25	485.16	19.101	19		3			1	19.102	0.001

 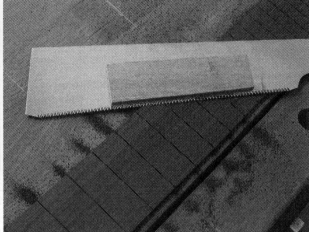

Cutting the fret slots   A taped-on depth stop ensures uniform slot depth

Cutting the fret slots

Guide your saw with the help of a square when cutting the fret slots. Don't forget to attach a strip of wood to the underside of the square (use double-faced tape) to ensure that the square touches the blade above the teeth of the saw. This is more accurate and prevents the teeth from rubbing against steel and thus dulling.

First cut off the fretboard at the zero-fret and the 25th fret. Then cut all the slots to a depth of 3/32" (2mm) before attaching a depth stop to the saw blade and deepening the slots to 1/8" (3mm). The depth stop, which is a thin piece of wood attached parallel to and at a distance of 1/8" (3mm) from the tips of the saw teeth helps to ensure equal slot depth.

Remove any saw marks with a scraper and deepen the slots again where neccessary.

Fitting the fretboard dot markers

This is done in the same way as described in Project One. Mark a center line along the fretboard and find the centers between two frets by scribing one line diagonally across the fret fields. The dot markers and the bit you use for drilling the cavities have to be of the same diameter (in my case 6mm). Since it is easier to sand the small dots flush than the entire fretboard surface, let the dots protrude a little when gluing them in. I used 1/16"(1.5mm)-thick dots, so I drilled to a depth of 0.050" (1.3mm). I did the drilling by hand, frequently checking the depth with a caliper. It wasn't difficult to get the depth of the cavities right. You have much more control over things when drilling by hand instead of using a handheld power drill.

For gluing in the dots combine two equal amounts of epoxy resin and hardener; use a type with an open time of several hours. Put a small amount into a cavity and press the dot in with the help of a dowel stick and a small hammer. Tap on the stick only very gently to not break the fragile inlay dots. Wipe off any excess glue with a damp rag and leave the epoxy to harden for at least 12 hours before flush-sanding the dots with 120-grit sandpaper. I used

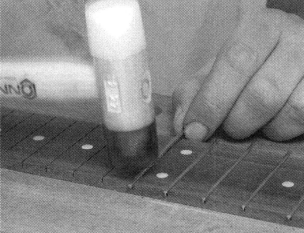

Drilling the recesses for the inlay dots   Hammering in the frets

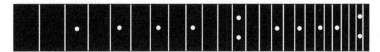

Arrangement of
fretboard dots

larger, 6mm-diameter dots for this guitar as the frets are further apart. Let the epoxy set
overnight, then sand the dots flush with 120-grit paper.

Installing the frets

The simplest method of fretting is to hammer the frets in, ideally with a soft-face hammer
to not mar the fret crowns. You need 24 pieces of fretwire, each roughly 2⁶/₈" (70mm) long.
When installing a fret, tap it in at one end first, then hammer across the fret slot until the
whole fret is seated well. The fret ends should not be loose or move when you push or pull
at them with your fingers.
I bought a set of 24 pieces of straight fretwire. Generally speaking, however, it is advisable to
use bent fretwire (even on flat fretboard surfaces) as it makes the fret ends stay in the slots
much better.

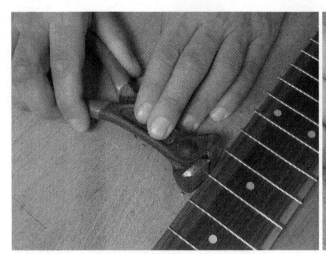
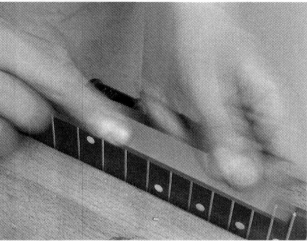

Cutting the frets flush with a fret-end nipper   Cutting the frets flush with a mill file

Cutting the fret ends flush

Cut the protruding fret ends flush with the sides of the fretboard. There are special fret-end cutters available from luthiers' suppliers which cut at the very tip so that less material is left protruding after the cut. By removing the front bevels of a wire cutter you can also make a fret-end flush-cutter yourself. I used a stationary disc sander for removing the front bevel of the cutter shown above. After cutting a lot of fretwire its cutting edge is still sharp. Even with a flush-cutter some material will always be left; this can be removed with a fine file. Keep filing until the rattling noise turns into a smooth sound.

To prevent the ends from popping up in future they ought to be glued down. Place a clamping caul on the frets and press it all down with several clamps. Turn the guitar on its side and apply a drop of thin CA glue to the ends. The glue will hopefully flow all across the slots; if necessary, repeat the procedure from the other side. Leave the guitar alone for several hours, then remove the clamps.

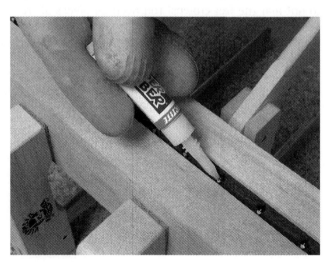

Applying thin CA glue
to the fret slot ends

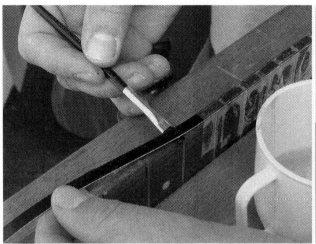
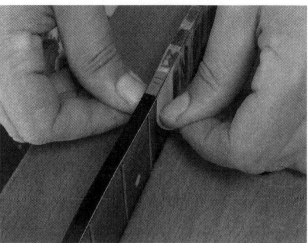

Applying acetone

Securing the binding with tape

Binding the fretboard

This step is optional. You can also leave the fretboard unbound and fill any fret slots that are too deep by putting a drop of PVA glue on the slot ends and then sanding the side of the fretboard: the wood dust will mix with the glue and fill the slots.

I decided to use a black-white-black celluloid binding because it adds a touch of elegance. If possible, use a binding of exactly the same height as the fretboard is thick. You can scrape the binding to the desired height by clamping it between two battens of the same height and length as the fretboard. Keep scraping until the tool touches the wood and you'll get a uniform binding height.

I didn't do this, so I had to cut the binding flush later, which is more work. Generously apply acetone to a small section of the binding and fretboard side. Press the binding on and secure it with tape as firmly as possible. If the tape breaks, use a second strip of tape on top of the

first one. The tape will automatically center the binding on the edge of the fretboard. After gluing on the binding on both sides, wait at least six hours before removing the tape.

Which glue should I use?

When you buy binding material from a guitarmakers' supplier, it is normally made of celluloid. The best solvent to use for gluing on such an acetate binding is acetone. Use CA glue for other types of binding.

Wait at least six hours before removing the tape

Cutting the binding flush with the fretboard surface | A fretboard cut-off serves as a height gauge

Cutting the binding flush

If your binding is not flush with the fretboard surface, cut it flush with a chisel. It helps a lot if you put a fretboard cut-off to the side to serve as a height gauge (especially in the fretwire areas). As I have already mentioned, it is much easier to scrape the binding to the correct height before gluing it on.

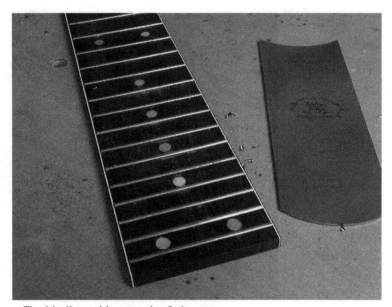

The binding adds a touch of elegance

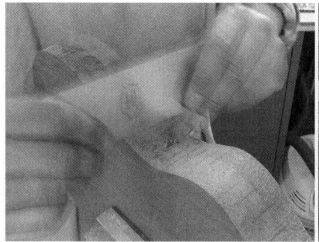
Scraping the sides of the body

Sanding the body sides

Binding the body

Smoothing the body sides

Before cutting the body binding rebate, square and smooth the sides as well as you can. Use a square and a pencil again to mark high spots, then remove them with a scraper. Repeat this until almost no light shines through between the surface and the square. Use the scraper in the direction of the grain only. Finally, sand the sides of the body with a sanding block and 120-grit followed by 180-grit sandpaper. Wrap the sandpaper around a tube or round bar when sanding in the concave waist areas of the body.

Cutting the binding rebate

Cutting by hand
You can cut the binding rebate by hand using a special purfling cutter and a small chisel. Such purfling cutters are available from guitarbuilders' suppliers. They consist of a handle with a guide pin and an adjustable cutter blade. Set the distance between the blade and the guide pin to a hair less than the width of the binding. Additionally, the blade must be adjusted so that it protrudes from the tool only by the height of the binding. Cut all around the body, making sure that the guide pin stays in contact with the side of the body all the time. Deepen the cut in several passes until the blade has fully entered the wood.
For the second cut adjust the distance between the blade and the guide pin to the height of the binding. Also adjust the blade so that it protrudes from the tool only by the width of the binding. Cut all the way around, keeping the guide pin in contact with the surface of the body. Remove the material between the two cuts with a small chisel.

Rebate cutter with interchangeable ball–bearings

Routing the binding rebate

Stop block

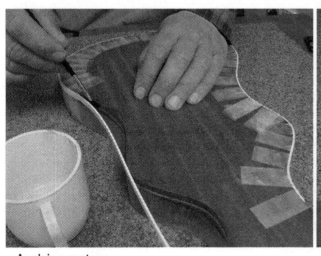

Applying acetone

The finished rebate

Remove the tape after 6 hours

Using a router

I became untrue to my principles and used a router for cutting the binding rebate. If you have access to one, a router will not only speed up the operation but also make it foolproof. The best cutter for this job is a special rebate cutter with interchangeable ball-bearings. The cutter shown on the facing page has a ¼" shaft and is available from *Wealden Tools*, a British company which ships worldwide (just in case you can't find such cutters near you). The depth of the rebate is defined by the ball-bearing and determined by the difference between the radii of the cutter and the ball-bearing. My cutter is 21mm in diameter, the ball-bearings are interchangeable and are sold seperately. The selection shown on the facing page will give you a cutting depth ranging from 1mm to 6.5mm (in 0.5mm steps). Although it's good to have them, you don't need all the bearings but only the one that is closest to the thickness of your binding. For my binding, which is 1.8mm thick, I used the 18mm bearing (21 minus 18 equals 3; 3 divided by 2 is 1.5mm). The binding will, and actually should, be a little wider and higher than the rebate so that it can be scraped flush once it has been glued on.

Clamp a stop board for the base of the router across the neck to make the cutter start and stop at the 12th fret. Start on the left side and cut the rebate in a counterclockwise direction until the baseplate of the router reaches the stop. Repeat the procedure to make sure that the rebate is uniformly deep all around.

Gluing on the binding

Like the fretboard binding the celluloid binding is also glued on with acetone. Generously apply acetone to a small section of the binding and rebate. Press the binding into the rebate and secure it with tape as firmly as possible. If the tape breaks, use two layers of tape on top of each other. Continue section by section and use some extra tape in the waist area, where the binding is most likely to come loose. Apply acetone to sections no longer than the width of your hand. Choose a section length that suits your working speed so that both binding and wood are still wet when pressed together. When you have finished, leave the tape on for at least six hours. Since the tape gets harder to remove the longer it is left on, you should take it off the following day. If you discover any weak joints, re-apply acetone to the seam and tape down the binding again in that section. If you have applied sufficient acetone and have used enough tape and force, the binding is going to bond very well to the wood.

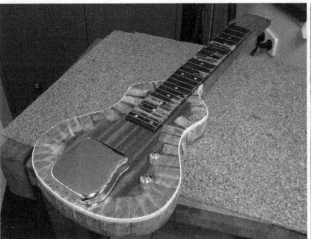

I couldn't resist the temptation of assembling the guitar provisionally at this stage

Scraping the binding flush

Scraping the binding flush

With a scraper, scrape the binding flush with the side of the body. Make sure to hold the edge of the scraper strictly parallel to the side. The binding is softer than the wood, so be careful to not remove too much material and to not make the binding thinner than necessary.

Gluing on the fretboard

Please refer to Project One for this step. Remember that the glue film is very slippery and that you have to prevent the fretboard from moving when tightening the clamps. To leave room for the nut, the fretboard should be placed about 1/4" (6mm) from the line where the peghead angle starts. I put the clamping block directly onto the frets. Two small blocks of wood clamped to the body will help to keep the fretboard aligned, but don't rely on that as the force of the clamps can move them together with the fretboard.

Gluing on the fretboard

Place the bridge at the end of the body so that the cover leaves the binding visible

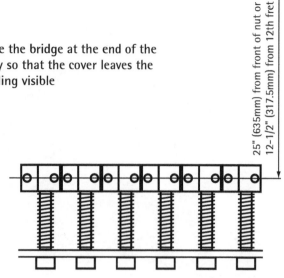

How the six saddles have to be adjusted

25" (635mm) from front of nut or
12-1/2" (317.5mm) from 12th fret

Mounting the bridge

Remove the saddles and put the cover on the *Tele*-style bridge. Place it at the end of the body so that the binding remains visible, then remove the cover. Center the bridge on the body center line and mark the centers of the six mounting holes. The saddles of this bridge are adjustable and will be adjusted to the scale length later on (see illustration above). For now, make sure that the bridge is centered and sits at the end of the body. I assume that the fretboard was glued on perfectly centered on the guitar centerline. If not, don't despair - it's more important to have the bridge centered on the fretboard. You can place a rule on both sides of the fretboard (thus artificially extending its edges to the bridge area) and then center the bridge on those two lines. Pre-drill the six screw holes with a 3/32"(2.5mm) twist drill bit and fasten the bridge with the supplied screws or with six 5/32" x 3/4"(4x20mm) wood screws with countersunk head.

Marking the
string mounting holes

Drilling the string
mounting holes

Making the string mounting holes

On a *Tele*-style bridge the strings are mounted from the back of the body. This requires the drilling of six ⅛"(3mm) holes through the body. Start with a twist drill bit, using the bridge holes as a template (see picture on previous page). Then remove the bridge and drill all six holes through the body. I did the drilling by hand, with good results: only two out of six holes were misplaced because I had not held the drill perfectly vertically. It should be possible to get all the holes right if you use some sort of drill guide. I plugged the two badly-positioned holes with a piece cut off a ⅛"(3mm) dowel and then marked new centers. The ball-ends of the strings will bear against string ferrules which require ½"(12mm)-deep holes, ⁵/₁₆" (8mm) in diameter. The string ferrules will be tapped in after the finish has been applied.

Considering that I drilled by hand the alignment of the holes is not so bad. I've seen
worse results produced on drill presses

Pre-drilling the pickup cavity

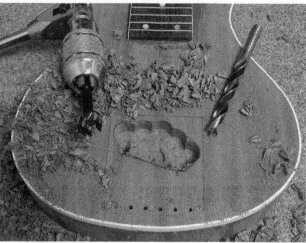

The pre-drilled pickup cavity

Removing material with a chisel

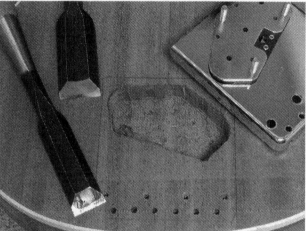

The finished pickup cavity

Cutting the cavities

Cutting the pickup cavity

Mount the bridge again and mark the outline of the bridge pickup opening and the centers of the three pickup mounting holes on the body; then remove the bridge again. Align the *Telecaster* bridge pickup on the three mounting hole marks and trace the outline of its base onto the body. Pre-drill the $^{19}/_{32}$"(15mm)-deep cavity with a $^{3}/_{4}$"(20mm) Forstner bit. Use a smaller bit for the tighter radii and a chisel for removing the remaining material. Mount the pickup on the bridge and check if everything can be fitted correctly.

After mounting the bridge

Marking the holes for the control pots

Pre-drilling the control cavity

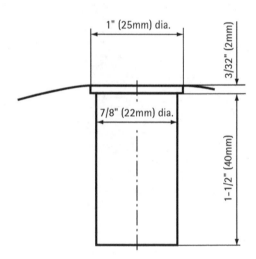
Output jack hole at the side of the body

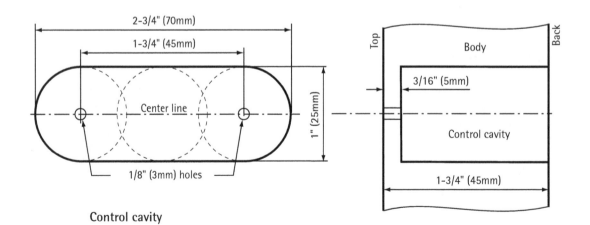
Control cavity

The output jack hole with jack mount

Connecting the pickup cavity with the control cavity

Cutting the control cavity

Place the potentiometer knobs on the body in the places you've chosen and mark their out-lines. Their centers should be 1³/4" (45mm) apart. Drill one ¹/8"(3mm) hole through the body at each knob center mark. Turn the guitar over, center the 1"(25mm) Forstner bit on one of the ¹/8"(3mm) holes and start to drill. To be able to mount the potentiometer there must not be more than ³/16" (5mm) of material left at the bottom of the hole. If the body is 1³/4" (1¹²/16") thick, you'll have to drill 1⁹/16" deep (1¹²/16"-1⁹/16"=³/16"). If the body is 44mm thick, you'll need to drill 39mm deep (44-39=5mm). Do the same with the other ¹/8"(3mm) hole before drilling a third hole in the middle. You can make this hole a little less deep so that the bottom of the control cavity is more rigid. Remove the remaining material between the holes with a chisel. I made the cover of the control cavity from ³/32"(2mm)-thick ebony veneer.

Cutting the output jack hole

The jack mount I used is held in place by two angled screws and is centered on the side of the body. I couldn't find a Forstner bit for the required ⁷/8"(22mm) hole, so I had to use the fairly large drill bit shown above. To give the jack mount a flat surface on the curved side of the body I drilled a ³/32"(2mm)-deep hole with a 1"(25mm) Forstner bit. The rest of the hole is ⁷/8" (22mm) in diameter and about 1¹/2" (40mm) deep. I managed to meet the end of the control cavity, so I didn't need to drill a separate connecting channel.

Drilling the connection hole

The connection between the control cavity and the pickup cavity is made with a long, ¹/4" to ⁵/16" (6-8mm) drill bit. Start as flat as possible and at the right angle to ensure that the bit really enters the electronic cavity or output jack cavity. If necessary, also drill a hole to con-nect the control cavity to the output jack hole.

Cutting the sides almost flush with a spokeshave

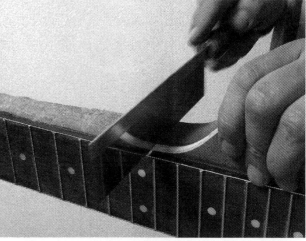

Cutting the step at the 12th fret

Cutting the sides flush with the chisel

Smoothing the sides with a scraper

Smoothing the back with a scraper

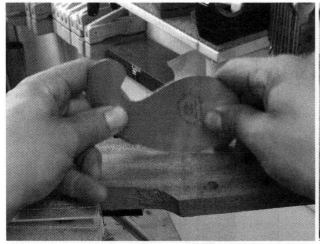

Smoothing the transition from the neck to the back of the peghead

Smoothing the transition from the neck to the side of the peghead

Cutting and smoothing the neck

Use a spokeshave to cut the sides of the neck almost flush with the fretboard; then finish the job with a wide chisel. Using a square, check if the sides of the neck are square to the fretboard and mark any high spots. Finally smooth both sides of the neck with a scraper. I made a small step at the 12th fret to visually separate the body from the neck (see photos on facing page and drawing below). Also smooth the back of the neck, the transition to the peghead and the back of the peghead. The peghead can be between 1/2" and 5/8" (13-15mm) thick.

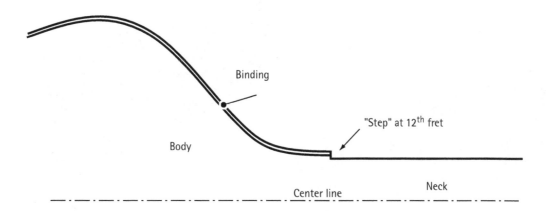

Binding

"Step" at 12th fret

Body

Center line

Neck

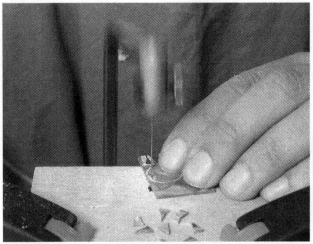

Cutting out the individual inlay pieces

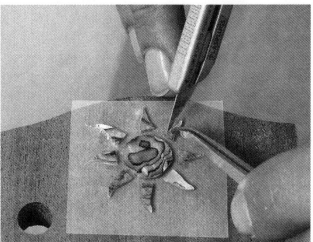

Transferring the outlines onto the wood

Cutting the cavities with a fine bit

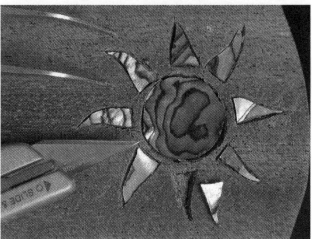

Fitting the inlay pieces into the cavities

The glued-in inlay after flush-sanding

The finished inlay

94

Inlaying

Cutting the inlay pieces

Cut out the individual pieces of your artistic drawing with a pair of scissors, glue them onto a shell blank and then cut them out again with the pearl cutting saw, brushing away the saw dust regularly. For making a cutting board drill a ¼"(6mm) hole near the edge of a piece of plywood and saw a narrow V-shaped kerf up to the hole (see picture on page 66). Hold down very small pieces with a pair of tweezers. If necessary, smooth the edges of the inlay pieces with a small file.

Safety measures
Shell dust (as any dust) is bad for your lungs. Even the small amounts an amateur guitarbuilder produces do matter, so always wear a face mask when cutting shell material or use some kind of dust collection that removes the dust right above and below the cutting board.

Cutting the inlay cavities

Glue a piece of paper on the area of the peghead where you want the inlay to be. Arrange the inlay pieces on the paper and glue them on with CA glue. Using a fine razor knife cut the outlines of the individual inlay pieces into the wood. To keep them from slipping about, hold them down with a small stick or a pair of tweezers. Deepen the cuts in several passes before carefully removing the inlay pieces with a chisel; the paper layer between wood and pearl makes it easy to do this. Lightly scrape away any paper residue before rubbing some chalk into the cut lines to improve visibility on the dark wood.

A tool often used for cutting inlay cavities is the *Dremel Mototool* with a base. Adjust the cutting depth to about 1/32" (1mm) and remove most of the material inside the outlines. Some sort of dust collection would come in very handy, otherwise you'll have to constantly blow away the dust in order to see what you are doing. Remove what is left near the cut lines with a knife. Set the router's cutting depth to a hair less than the thickness of the inlay pieces and repeat the steps above. Try if the inlay pieces already fit into the cavities; cut around them where necessary. While it is a sign of good craftsmanship if you fit the pieces in as tightly as possible, you can also make more-generously-sized cavities and then fill them with black epoxy filler (especially if you want a black peghead).

Gluing in the inlays

Mix some epoxy and blacken it by adding ebony saw dust. Put the black epoxy into the cavities and press the inlay pieces in. Put a piece of paper on the inlays and use a clamp and a small clamping caul to gently press the inlays down. Remove the caul after 12 hours and sand off any squeezed-out epoxy with 80-grit sandpaper wrapped around a sanding block. As soon as the surface is almost level, switch to 120-grit paper to not unnecessarily scratch the inlays. Finish with a scraper. I'm not an expert in the art of inlaying, but as the picture shows, even a mediocre inlaying job can look pretty acceptable after sanding and finishing.

A must-read for everyone interested in inlay work is
"The Art of Inlay" by *Larry Robinson*.

| The nut is installed in a recess | Rounding over the edges with 180-grit sandpaper |

Installing the nut

The nut, a small piece of ebony in the dimensions 3/16" x 5/8" x 27/16" (5x15x62mm), is installed in a small recess at the end of the fretboard. Push the nut to the fretboard end and scribe its width on the neck with a fine knife. Saw two 1/8"(3mm)-deep kerfs, one on either side of the nut, and then remove the material in between with a small chisel. The nut should fit tightly into this recess into which it will be glued later on.

Finishing

Final sanding of the guitar

Start with 80-grit sandpaper on a sanding block and sand the whole guitar except the inlay area, in the direction of the grain. Lightly round over the edges with a small piece of sandpaper, then switch to 120-grit. Carefully remove the sanding dust with a brush before finishing with 180-grit paper.

Filling the mahogany pores

This guitar will be finished with varnish. In order to get a smooth surface on an open-pored timber like mahogany it is necessary to first fill the pores of the wood with paste wood filler, which is a mixture of ground stone (silica) and a binder (such as varnish). I would recommend using an oil-based filler. Water-based fillers are also available, but they are more difficult to apply as they dry very fast. When using a waterbase filler, only work on a small area at a time and remove any excess immediately. Always use a filler that is darker in color than the surrounding wood as otherwise the filled pores will be too light and will give the guitar a speckled appearence. I used a medium-mahogany-color filler, which I applied directly to the

Applying the paste wood filler

The fretboard is protected with taped-on paper

bare wood so that the wood was also stained in the process. If you just want to fill the pores without changing the color of the wood, you have to apply a sealer coat before putting on the filler.

The filler must have the consistency of heavy cream and can be applied with a plastic spreader or a cheap brush. Round off the edges of the spreader to prevent it from scratching the wood. Smear the paste on, then work the filler into the pores by moving the spreader in all directions. After several minutes you'll notice that the filler coat is starting to dry. As soon as it becomes dull (looking like dry mud), remove as much of the remaining filler as possible with the plastic spreader or a coarse rag, working across the grain. Follow up with a coarse rag, again wiping across the grain to avoid pulling out filler from the pores.

Wait until the next day before lightly sanding the surface with 180-grit sandpaper, and wait for at least another two days before applying the finish. The pore filler needs to be left to dry completely, or else you'll be in serious trouble.

Scraping the binding

You can make your own binding scraper from a small block of wood, a cutter blade and a bolt

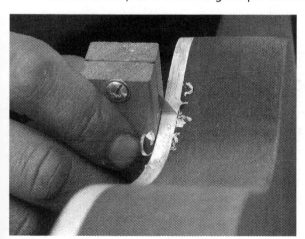

with nut as shown in the illustration below. The blade is clamped in the kerf by tightening the bolt. Adjust the blade so that it protrudes from the block of wood by the height of the binding and then scrape the binding clean as in the picture on the left. Scrape only lightly to avoid removing too much material.

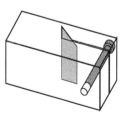

Scraping the binding clean

Applying the finish

There's one golden rule for achieving a flawless finish: avoid dust. If possible, don't use the same room for sanding and finishing. If, however, you have no choice and, like me, are forced to do all your work in one room, it's essential to wait at least an hour after the last sanding session to give the dust some time to settle. Varnish remains sticky for at least an hour, and any dust in the air would settle on the wet finish.

Holding the guitar during finishing

One practical problem that occurs during finishing is how to hold the guitar so that the wet finish can dry without being touched. My solution is to clamp the neck into a vise with soft protection cauls and to first finish the top and the sides of the body and the peghead. Half an hour later I turn the guitar over and finish the back. After another 30 minutes I stick a bolt through one of the top tuner holes and put a nut on the end of the bolt. Then I hang the bolt (and with it the guitar) into two hooks mounted on the ceiling. This way I can finish both sides of the neck and the fretboard and still leave the whole guitar to dry completely without touching it. I finish the frets with varnish too.

Preparing the brush

Before you first use your brush remember to remove any loose bristles by hitting the bristles against the palm of your hand. Always condition the brush by dipping the bristles into a thinner for several seconds. This will make it much easier to clean the brush after use.

Hanging the guitar for drying

98

Storing the brush beetween coats

When you're finished for the day, brush the remaining finish on a clean sheet of paper. Dip the brush into the quarter-filled jar, then wipe the bristles clean with a rag. Most finishers recommend that you clean the brush completely every day in order to keep the bristles in good shape (see below). I'm rather lazy and do this only once - when the guitar is finished. A finishing session usually lasts several days; during this time I keep the brush stored in a second jar halfway filled with balsam turpentine. I put a lid with an opening for the brush handle on the jar so the solvent has less of a chance to evaporate. The bristles must hang clear of the bottom of the jar; a small clamp, such as a clothespin, can serve as a depth stop. When the jar is no longer needed, I put a new lid on, label it clearly ("Balsam turpentine/Storage") and keep the jar and the lid with the opening stored in a safe place for finishing the next guitar with the same varnish. I also label the jar used for cleaning the brush ("Balsam turpentine/Wash") and also store it until it is needed the next time. I think this is an enviromentally-friendly approach; it only requires adding some thinner when the liquid level in the jars is low. Impurities will sink to the bottom of the jar after some time. By carefully pouring the thinner into another jar you can keep the balsam turpentine clean enough to fulfill its purpose.

Thorough cleaning of the brush

You can clean the brush thorougly every day or, like me, only once, after the last coat of finish. I always wear gloves for this. Remove most of the remaining finish from the bristles by brushing it onto paper; then put the bristles into a thinner and squeeze and massage them with your fingers. Next, wipe the bristles dry with a clean rag. Repeat this procedure twice, then put some drops of washing-up liquid on the bristles and work them into the bristles with your fingers. Continue for several minutes, then rinse the brush. Repeat this step twice before wrapping the bristles in paper and storing the brush away. You don't need to have tap water in your workshop; a bucket and a water canister with tap are all you need.

Applying the varnish

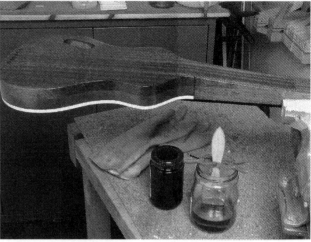
The body is left to dry before the neck is finished

Leveling a coat of varnish

Leveling the last coat after one week of drying

Putting on a buffing compound

Buffing the varnish to a shine

Finishing schedule

Day one
Mix one part of oil-based varnish with one part of turpentine and brush on a sealer coat.

Day two
Brush on the first coat of oil varnish. Don't use it full-strength, right out of the can, but thin the varnish with about 10 percent of thinner. Start at some distance from an edge and slowly brush towards that edge. Then lift the brush back to the starting point and slowly apply the varnish towards the opposite edge. This way you'll never move the bristles over an edge (which would produce runs on the sides). When you approach an edge, lift the brush like a plane taking off. Do the brushing ve-e-e-ry slowly; the varnish should be constantly flowing off the brush and leave an evenly-thick film on the wood. Finish the surface section by section and with great patience and care. Although varnish dries very slowly and therefore levels itself, it pays off to apply it very carefully.

Day three
Level the entire surface by lightly sanding it with 400-grit silicone-carbide paper. If there are any varnish drops or runs on the surface, cut them level with a chisel. Avoid sanding through the finish and take special care at the edges. Remove all sanding dust and - if you do the finishing in the same room - let the dust settle for at least an hour before applying the second coat.

Day four
Level the entire surface again, this time with 400-grit paper. Carefully remove the dust, then apply a third coat.

Next few days
Apply further coats as described above (4 to 6 coats should be sufficient). After the last coat leave the guitar alone for at least a week. The varnish is too soft for polishing now, so busy yourself with something else - for example, start making the case.

One week later: final rub-out
Level the varnished surface with 600-grit wet-or-dry paper on a small cork sanding block, using water as a lubricant. Check against the light and at different angles if there are any shiny spots on the surface, i.e. spots which are lower than most of the surface and have not yet been touched by the sandpaper. Minimize the number of these shiny spots by further sanding. Clean the surface frequently with a rag. Be very careful, for if you sand through to the bare wood in only one small spot, you'll have to apply another coat of varnish (and to unwrap the already-cleaned brush again!). After two or three days such a newly-applied thin coat should have cured well enough to allow continuing. When almost all the shiny spots have disappeared, switch to 1200-grit wet-or-dry paper.

Buffing the guitar
Smear some buffing compound on the surface and buff it to a shine using a soft cloth. Work in all directions and apply some force in order to get a satisfactory result. Wipe off any residue when you have finished.

Wire, bobbin, bolts, springs
and metal baseplate for a
Tele-style bridge pickup

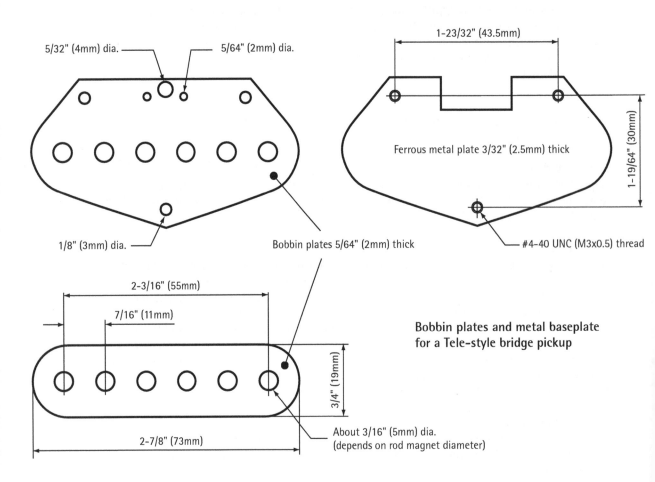

5/32" (4mm) dia.

5/64" (2mm) dia.

1/8" (3mm) dia.

Bobbin plates 5/64" (2mm) thick

1-23/32" (43.5mm)

Ferrous metal plate 3/32" (2.5mm) thick

1-19/64" (30mm)

#4-40 UNC (M3x0.5) thread

2-3/16" (55mm)

7/16" (11mm)

3/4" (19mm)

2-7/8" (73mm)

About 3/16" (5mm) dia.
(depends on rod magnet diameter)

Bobbin plates and metal baseplate
for a Tele-style bridge pickup

Making the pickup

You can use any *Tele*-style bridge pickup for this project, or you can make the entire pickup yourself following the instructions below.

Making the pickup bobbin

There are ready-made pickup bobbins available; for a list of suppliers please refer to my website. You can also make the bobbin plates yourself by using 3/32"(2mm)-thick solid wood or plywood or several layers of black cardboard glued together with black epoxy. Using plastic material is not a good idea because it will melt when heated during soldering. An ideal material for making pickup bobbins is *Forbon*™, a brand name for vulcanized fiberboard, which comes in 4x8ft sheets.
You should be able to get the magnets in electronics stores as Alnico magnets of the required size - about 3/16" (5mm) in diameter and 3/4" (20mm) long - are used to operate reed switches. The six magnets are press-fitted into the bobbin plates and can be secured additionally with thin CA glue.

ALNICO
Alnico is an artificial, permanently-magnetic material consisting of a mixture of ALuminum, NIckel and CObalt. Depending on composition and strength, Alnico magnets are named differently, Alnico 5 being the best-known of these mixtures.

Getting the wire

You need 0.06mm-thick insulated copper wire for winding the pickup. This type of wire is commonly called AWG42 (AWG = American Wire Gauge). It is used for winding small electric motors, so one place to ask for it would be at a local motor repair shop. Or you could also try your luck at different electronics stores. Fortunately, it has become easier to get pickup coil wire as it is now available from some larger guitarbuilders' suppliers (check my website for addresses).
I bought my wire directly from a wire manufacturer for about $55 per kilogram (2 pounds). They offered to wind the required length onto a smaller bobbin, but I decided to buy the large quantity (which will probably last me a lifetime). With 2 pounds (1 kilogram) of wire you should be able to wind around 25 single-coil pickups! Using thicker wire would not leave enough space on the coil for the number of windings needed, and the use of thinner wire would result in d.c. resistance becoming excessively high, which would make the pickup sound less clear.

Some wire data

AWG	Diameter	D.c. resistance	Recommended tension
42	0.0025"	1.66 ohms/feet	1.2 ounces
	(0.063mm)	(5.4 ohms/meter)	(33 grams)

Probably the world's simplest pickup winder

A hand drill and some easy-to-get materials are all you need

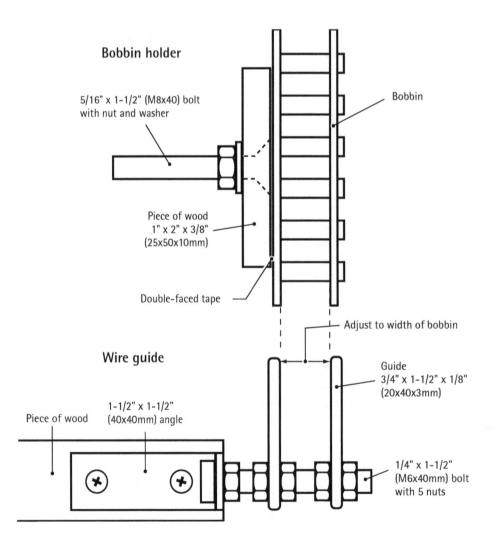

Bobbin holder

5/16" x 1-1/2" (M8x40) bolt
with nut and washer

Bobbin

Piece of wood
1" x 2" x 3/8"
(25x50x10mm)

Double-faced tape

Adjust to width of bobbin

Wire guide

Guide
3/4" x 1-1/2" x 1/8"
(20x40x3mm)

Piece of wood

1-1/2" x 1-1/2"
(40x40mm) angle

1/4" x 1-1/2"
(M6x40mm) bolt
with 5 nuts

Making a pickup winder

My pickup winder is as simple as it can get: a hand drill clamped horizontally into a vise turns the bobbin. Please note that not all hand drills can be clamped as directly as mine. By mounting the drill on a block of wood you should, however, be able to clamp other types too. One quarter-turn of the crank equals one complete turn of the bobbin, so the ratio is 1:4. You can substitute the hand drill with a cordless drill, an electric drill or an electric motor, but that way you'll never get the fine, almost infinite control of winding by hand which allows you to stop immediately at any time.

Winding the pickup

Preparing the bobbin
To prevent wire breakage, round over the inside edges of the bobbin plates with 400-grit sandpaper. The surfaces and edges have to be as smooth as possible as the wire will get entangled at the smallest of imperfections. My bobbin came with solder lugs and looked ready for winding. So I started and put on several hundreds of turns; then the wire got caught at the edges of the eyelets and I had to cut it off and file and sand the eyelets flush to the bobbin-plate surface. If you want to avoid this problem, remove the eyelets before you start winding.

Mounting the bobbin
I used a small piece of wood [1" x 2" x 3/8" (25x50x10mm)] as a base for mounting the bobbin. Drill a hole into the center and fix a countersunk bolt as illustrated on the facing page. Center the bobbin on the base and fasten it with strong double-faced tape. Don't use the thin type of double-faced tape for this which you see me using in this book, but take the thicker type which is made for fastening mirrors.

Starting
Wind several turns on the bobbin, bend the starting end of the wire over the edge of the baseplate and tape it down. Start turning the bobbin slowly; bear in mind that you have to put on around 8000 turns. If you assume one crank turn per second, it will take 2000 seconds to wind the complete pickup (8000:4). This means that, theoretically, you will be finished in a reasonable 33 minutes. In practice, however, it is going to take longer as you'll have to stop and check the windings regularly. So why not divide the winding job into four sessions of 10 minutes each and take a break after each session to remain concentrated? Hold the wire between your thumb and index finger. The friction thus created will give just the right amount of wire tension to prevent the wire from breaking or being wound on too loose, the latter inevitably making the pickup prone to feedback. The recommended tension for AWG42 wire is 1.2 ounces (33 grams).

Feedback
Feedback occurs when you place a microphone near a loudspeaker: the ambient noise is picked up by the microphone, gets amplified and then re-transmitted by the speaker. The sound from the speaker is then picked up again by the microphone and re-amplified and re-transmitted. This builds up in no time at all and produces a loud and extremely unpleasant noise. A good pickup acts only as a "microphone" for the moving strings. But as soon as the coil wire is able to move (as a result of the vibrations of the incoming

The winder in action

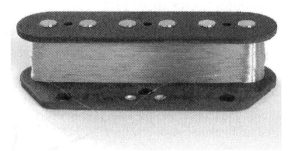

This coil has a d.c. resistance reading of 5.9K ohms

soundwaves), it also induces a signal that gets amplified immediately. The soundwaves from the speaker cause the wire to move even more, and this, in turn, creates an even stronger signal, which is amplified again. The result is really bad feedback. A pickup with loose windings will feedback much earlier than a properly-wound one.

The thin wire is smooth and will not cut your skin, at least not as long as you wind by hand like me. Don't wear gloves as this makes you lose the fine control you have with your fingers. When I tried using cotton gloves the wire broke several times. If you work very carefully, you will be able to wind the whole coil without breaking the wire. If it should break, resist the temptation of trying to solder it together. This is one possibility and probably worth a thought if there are already several thousands of turns on the bobbin, but generally speaking it is safe to say that cutting off the wire with a knife and starting all over again is the easier way.

Guiding the wire

I have wound several pickups without wire guide, but always found that I was over-cautious near the sides of the coils where the wire can easily come off the bobbin. The coil should be wound evenly flat, without "bulk" in the middle. To minimize the risk of missing the bobbin I recommend that you fasten a simple wire guide (as shown on page 104) together with the drill. Set the inside of the guide so that it is level with the inside of the bobbin plates and you will wind with much more confidence. The edges of the guides have to be smoothed to prevent them from breaking the wire. Guide the wire in even movements from one side to the other while turning the bobbin. When you approach the other side, guide the wire back in the same way. Always apply a certain amount of finger pressure on the wire to keep it sufficiently tensioned. You can test if the wire is too loose by tapping on the coil with the tip of one of your fingers. There should be hardly any movement noticeable; the coil should lie right on the magnets.

Checking the resistance

When winding a pickup, I don't count the turns but check the coil's d.c. resistance. A *Telecaster* pickup typically has a d.c. resistance of 5.9 to 7K ohms (5900 to 7000 ohms); you can stop

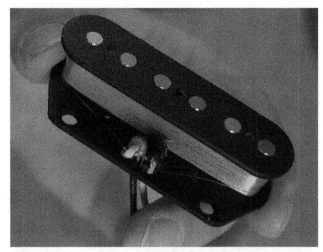

A genuinely hand-wound pickup

winding as soon as this resistance value is reached. Take the first measurement when the bobbin is about three-quarters full. Lift the wire out of the guide and hold it against the outside of the right wire guide. Carefully sand off the insulation in one spot - a few light strokes with a small piece of 400-grit paper are sufficient. Take care or the wire will break and force you to start all over again. Do the same at the starting end of the coil. Switch your multimeter to the 20K-range, then hold the probes to the blank wire spots. You should have a stable and reliable reading of several K ohms. If not, move the probe a bit, or, if this doesn't help either, sand lightly over the wire again. When I first measured, the resistance was 5.3K ohms. I continued winding and soon reached the goal of a d.c. resistance reading of 5.9K ohms.

Wiring the pickup

When the required resistance is shown, cut off the wire with a knife and remove the bobbin from the holder. Thread the wire ends through the eyelets and tension them by taping the wire to the back of the bobbin plate. Thread the pickup cables through the middle hole and stick each end into an eyelet. I also made a knot at the end of both cables to get better protection against pull. Another way of protecting the delicate solder points would be to hold the cable ends in place with small plastic cable binders. Heat the eyelets, then apply solder and keep the soldering iron a bit longer in contact than necessary (I slowly count to six). The heat should be sufficient to melt the pickup wire insulation. If your multimeter shows "OL", re-heat the solder points until you get the previous resistance reading of 5.9 to 7K ohms.

Placing a small cable binder above and another one below the baseplate prevents cable movement and stress on the solder joints

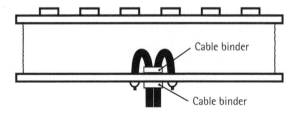

Cable binder

Cable binder

Immersing the coil in hot wax

Potting the pickup

A common method of fixing the wire on a coil is potting. Heat enough wax to allow immersing the whole pickup. To heat the wax evenly, put the wax pot into a water-filled container. Heat the wax to 150°F (65°C) and make sure it stays at that temperature throughout the potting process. Do not exceed this limit this temperature is sufficient and safe, whereas higher temperatures can damage the pickup. When the wax is hot, put the pickup in and leave it there for about 10 minutes. I tape a ¼"(6mm)-high "distance block" to the back of the pickup to ensure it stays at a certain minimum distance from the bottom of the pot. The wax in the photo is dark because I used the wax of a dark-green candle. Normally clear wax is used. If you want to make a special mix for potting your pickup, use a mixture of 80 percent paraffin and 20 percent beeswax; pure paraffin wax is too brittle, and pure beeswax has a melting point that is too low. By combining about one part of beeswax with four parts of paraffin wax you'll get a perfect mixture.

Safety measures
Hot paraffin and paraffin vapors can ignite, so be cautious and don't overheat the wax.
Have a lid within reach so you can quickly extinguish any potential fire.
Wear safety goggles when potting pickups.

I would not even dream of claiming that hand-wound pickups sound better than machine-made ones with their exact layers and perfect wire tension, but I find it "cool" to have a "genuinely hand-wound" pickup. If you want to automate the winding process, all you basically have to do is control the tension and the horizontal travel of the wire within very narrow borders. But building a machine really only pays off if you intend to wind more than the odd pickup every now and then. For the occasional, amateur guitarbuilder my method is more than adequate.

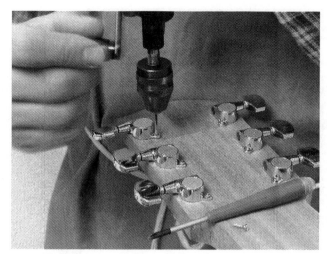
Drilling a hole for mounting a tuner

Assembling the guitar

Mount the tuners and tap the string ferrules into their holes at the back of the body. Use a small block of wood and a hammer for this.

Wiring the electronics

Circuit diagram
This guitar has a volume and tone control. The capacitor **C** on the tone pot acts as a "gateway" for the higher frequencies, which are more and more cut as the tone pot "wiper" is turned away from the open lug. Common values for tone control caps are .020 and .050mf (mf=microfarad), 0.050 µF (µF=microfarad outside the USA) or 50nF (nF=nanofarad).

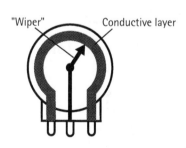

A pot is a variable resistor
(The middle lug is
connected to a "wiper")

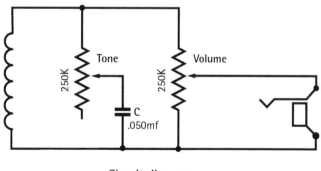

Circuit diagram

Mounted pickup: the ground wire makes contact with the metal plate via the pickup mounting bolt in the front

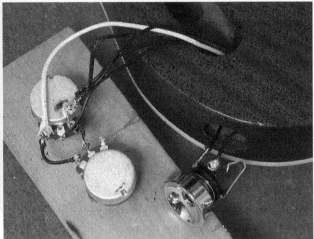

A board with two holes holds the pots during wiring

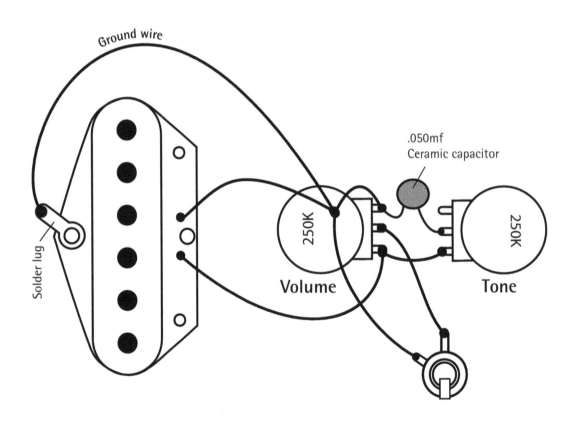

Wiring diagram: the components are shown from the back

Wiring

Solder a wire to the bottom of the pickup's metal plate, or fasten it together with a pickup fastening screw.

Push the two pickup wires and the ground wire through the connection channel into the control cavity. Mount the bridge on the body. Solder two wires to the output jack and push them into the control cavity, too. All the wires should be long enough to allow you to solder them to the pots outside the control cavity. I drilled two ¼"(6mm) holes into a board and stuck the pots in upside down, the distance between the holes there being the same as on the guitar. This way the electronics can be wired comfortably.

Some soldering tips

It doesn't matter which of the pickup wires you choose as the "live" one as long as there is only one pickup on the guitar.

Usually the output jack has one longer lug which is opposite the spring contact that touches the tip of the guitar cord plug. This is the "hot" lug that must be connected to the middle lug on the volume pot. The other lug is grounded on the volume pot case. Twist together and pre-tin the four wires that are to be connected to the case of the volume pot. Because the greater mass of the case makes it difficult to heat it, hold the wires on the pot and heat them together with the case of the pot for a bit longer than usual before applying the solder.

Mounting the electronics

When you have finished the wiring, stick the pots into their holes on the body and fix them by tightening the nuts. Arrange the wires in the control cavity, then close it with the cover and hope you will never have to open it again!

Stringing the guitar

Use a medium or heavy string gauge on lap steel guitars. Push the first string from the back through the body, stretch it over the bridge and the nut to the second tuner and make a sharp bend there. This ensures sufficient string is left for winding it three to four times around the tuner post. Thread the string up to the bend through the first tuner and start turning the peg while holding the string stretched with the other hand. Wind the string on the post so that each new layer is placed below the previous one. Do the same with the other strings. To get the required length reserve, always bend the strings towards the outside at the next tuner.

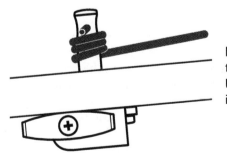

No more than four windings on the post and each new layer placed below the previous one: this is how it should be done!

Gluing on the nut

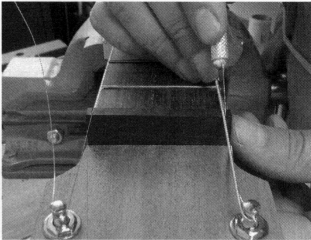

Scribing the string position

Slotting the nut

Final setup

Slotting the nut

The nut will not sit firmly in place unless it is glued on. Loosen the strings so that you can push three to either end of the nut. Remove the nut, sand its surface (if necessary) and round off the top outside edges with a fine file. Apply some CA glue to the front end of the fretboard and also to the bottom of the nut, then press the nut firmly into its place for about a minute. Place the strings on the nut so that they run parallel to the edge of the fretboard and, with a razor knife, cut small marks on either side of the outer strings into the top of the nut. Divide the distance between the outer strings by 5 and mark the nut slots for the other strings. If you want to have a correct-looking string spacing rather than a mathematically precise one, arrange the four inner strings without measuring, leaving more space between the bass strings

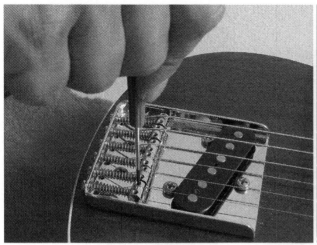

Adjusting the saddle height   Adjusting the pickup height

and putting the treble strings closer together. When you are happy with the distances, mark the string positions on the nut.

Use a fine saw for cutting shallow slots between the marks; then widen the bass string slots with your nut files. When finished, the tops of all the strings should be at the same height.

Slot the nut so that the tops of the strings are at an equal height

Adjust the saddles so that the tops of the strings are at an equal height

Saddle and pickup height adjustment

Adjust all the saddles to a distance of 25" (635mm) from the front of the nut. Alternatively, you can measure half the scale length, i.e. 22½" (317.5mm), from the middle of the 12th fret (see page 87). Press the bridge cover on the bridge and check how high the individual saddles can be set without making the strings touch the inside of the cover. Remove the cover again and set the saddles as high as possible, leaving about ¹/₁₆" (2mm) clearance for the strings' vibrations. Place the strings back on the nut, tune them to your favorite open tuning and - start playing!

You can set the pickup closer to the strings by turning the three mounting bolts in a clockwise direction. There should be a gap of about ⅛" (3mm) between the top of the polepieces and the bottom of the strings. Do not set it any closer than this as the magnetic force of the pickup would interfere with the free vibration of the strings and lead to intonation problems. Because of the way it is mounted, it is not possible to tilt a *Tele*-style bridge pickup.

Now that you have built the guitar, there is only one thing left to do: **play the thing!**

And if you haven't played a lap steel guitar before: **learn how to play the thing!**

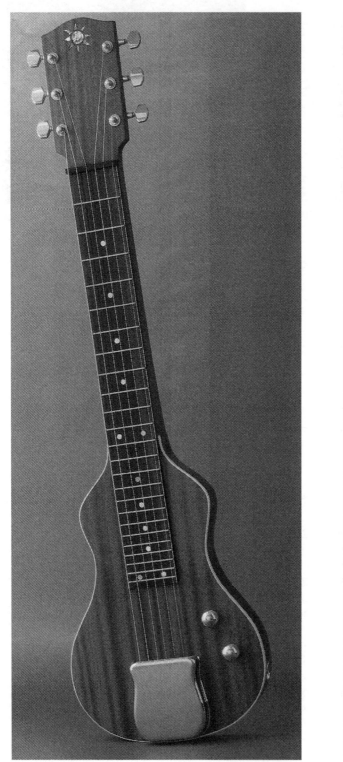

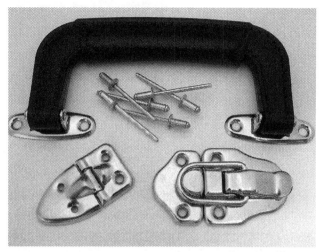

Case hardware

Making the case

Materials needed

2 35" x 3" (900x80mm) pieces of 1/4" (6mm) plywood
2 11" x 3" (280x80mm) pieces of 1/4" (6mm) plywood
2 35 3/8" x 11 3/4" (910x300mm) sheets of 5/32" (4mm) plywood or fiberboard
2 35" x 11 3/4" (900x300mm) foam sheets, 3/4" (20mm) thick
1 35" x 11 3/4" (900x300mm) foam sheet, 1/8" (3mm) thick
3 90-degree hinges
3 drawbolts
1 handle
20 5/32" (4mm) aluminum blind rivets for a material thickness of 5/16" (8mm)

Tools needed

6 clamps
Router with flush-cutting bit
Ryoba saw
Hand drill
5/32" (4mm) twist drill bit
Manual riveting tool

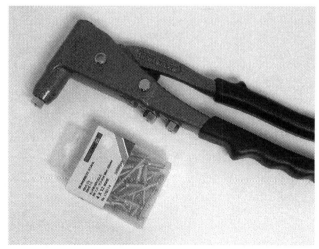

Manual riveting tool

Cutting the case top flush to the sides

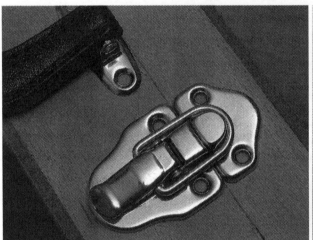

Marking the cutting line

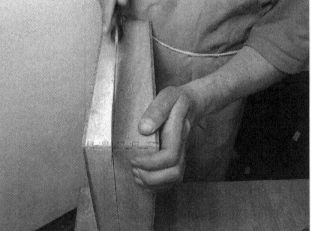

Cutting the case apart

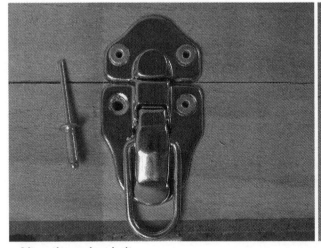

Mounting a drawbolt

A mounted hinge

The construction method is the same as in Project One, but this time I used 1/4"(6mm) plywood for the sides. I used fiberboard again for the top and back, but you can also use plywood instead. Use the same dowel-joint method as in Project One if you don't want to spend too much time making the case.

I took the time to make dovetail joints. Glue on the over-sized top and back with 6 clamps and PVA glue as shown in Project One and let the glue dry overnight. Cut the top and back of the case flush to the sides with a flush-cutting bit mounted on the router. Center a drawbolt on the side of the case and mark the point where the two drawbolt parts meet. Cut this mark all around with a marking gauge, then saw the case apart with a Ryoba saw and level the cut with a block plane if necessary.

The three hinges, the three locks and the handle are all fastened with blind rivets. I enlarged the holes of the locks to 5/32" (4mm). Hold the case together with two clamps and use a hinge or lock as a template for drilling; use a 5/32"(4mm) twist drill bit. Pull the handles of the manual riveting tool apart and insert a blind rivet. Stick the rivet into the hole and press the handles of the tool together. If necessary, open and press the handles together several times until the rivet tail breaks off. Do the same at the other mounting holes.

The most important thing to know when shopping for blind rivets is the material thickness range they are intended for. Note that this is not the length of the rivet head. Buy rivets that can be used for connecting parts of 5/16" (8mm) total thickness when using 1/4"(6mm)-thick material for the case.

Don't mount the handle in the middle, but position it at the balance point of the case because the body side of the instrument is heavier than the neck side. The case is padded with three layers of foam sheets. The bottom layer is 1/8" (3mm) thick; from the middle layer, which is 3/4" (20mm) thick, the guitar shape is cut out with a pair of scissors; the top layer in the lid of the case is also 3/4" (20mm) thick.

A simple instrument case

The middle foam layer is cut out to accept the guitar

Suppliers

The first thing to do when looking for tools and materials is to check what's available locally. If you can't get everything you need this way, there's always the World Wide Web and the websites of different mail order suppliers. Most suppliers ship worldwide and accept credit cards. There will be shipping costs, customs duties and taxes to pay, but sometimes you have no choice. It's safe to assume about 30 percent in additional costs when ordering from overseas.
Because suppliers come and go, I have decided to put all information about material suppliers on my website, where it will be updated regularly.

`www.BuildYourGuitar.com/lapsteel`

Simply log in with your user name and password (given at the beginning of this book) and find the addresses of all the suppliers mentioned in this book as well as direct links to products.

Common abbreviations

in	inch
"	inch
mm	millimeter
cm	centimeter
m	meter
kg	kilogram
dia.	diameter
l	liter
ft	feet
°	degree
F	Fahrenheit
C	Celsius
lb	pound
K ohms	kilo ohms
mf	microfarad
e.g.	for example
i.e.	that is
approx.	approximately

Unit conversions

1" = 25.4mm
1mm = 0.0394"
1 foot = 12" = 304.8mm
1 pound = 0.4536 kilograms
Celsius = (Fahrenheit - 32) / 1.8
Fahrenheit = Celsius x 1.8 + 32

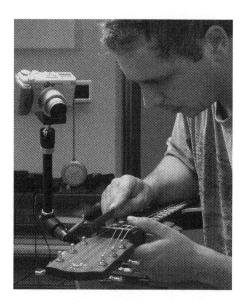

About the author

Martin Koch is a self-taught amateur guitarbuilder with three main interests: guitarbuilding, book design and writing instruction manuals. Luckily he can combine all of these in his self-published books. Having a daytime job and a family as well as being busy with his publishing activities he currently has little time left for building instruments other than those needed for his books. *It's easy to Build Your Own Lap Steel Guitar* is Martin Koch's second book in English. The author lives with his wife Brigitte and their three children in Austria.

Also by Martin Koch:
- Building Electric Guitars
- CD-ROM: Build Your Solid-Body Guitar

About this book

➡ The manuscript was typed on an *AlphaSmart 3000*, a simple but great portable text computer with USB interface.

➡ The book was created on a *Pentium 4*, 2GHz with 512MB RAM using *Adobe InDesign 2*, *Photoshop 6* and *Illustrator 9*.

➡ The fonts used are RotisSemisans, Schmalhans and TheSansTypewriter-Plain.

➡ All photos where taken by the author with a *Canon PowerShot G3*, 4 megapixel, digital camera using its rotating monitor and wireless remote control.

➡ The whole book was printed by *Lightningsource Inc.* using book-on-demand technology. Currently only black-and-white photos are possible, but you can find all the photos in color at www.BuildYourGuitar.com/lapsteel (see page 3 for details).

Lightning Source UK Ltd.
Milton Keynes UK
UKHW031330180319
339368UK00005B/259/P